John Henry

John Henry

by STEVE HASKIN

THOROUGHBRED
Legends®

No. 10

ECLIPSE
PRESS

Lexington, Kentucky

Library of Congress Card Number: 00-104788

ISBN 1-58150-058-0

Printed in The United States
First Edition: August 2001

a division of
The Blood-Horse, Inc.
PUBLISHERS SINCE 1916

To learn more about John Henry
and other classic Thoroughbreds, see:

www.thoroughbredlegends.com

JOHN HENRY

CONTENTS

JOHN HENRY

INTRODUCTION

Against All Odds

R on McAnally had never flown with John Henry before. To the ten-year-old gelding, this flight seemed no different than the thirty-plus flights he'd taken, other than the presence of his long-time trainer and friend. But McAnally knew this flight was very different. This time John Henry would not be coming home. So when horse transporter Tex Sutton invited McAnally and his wife, Debbie, to come along, free of charge, there was no hesitation.

As McAnally boarded Sutton's chartered Boeing 727 in Los Angeles, countless thoughts and memories swirled through his brain. He had only a few more hours to spend with John before the old boy was to be turned out at his new home at the Kentucky Horse Park outside Lexington.

For more than five years, John Henry was a major

part of McAnally's life, taking him from one adventure to another, while never ceasing to amaze the veteran trainer with his remarkable feats. Their bonding went far beyond that of horse and trainer. McAnally had spent his youth in an orphanage following the death of his mother and knew the feeling of being unwanted. John Henry, who McAnally would often say "came up from the ghetto," also was unwanted. McAnally took in this irascible youngster, who for the first four years of his life had been tossed around from one barn to another like unclaimed baggage, and showered him with kindness. Together they would make history.

Although John was now ten, the spark and eternal youthful spirit that carried him to thirty stakes victories (sixteen of them grade Is) and record earnings of $6,597,947 still shone brightly. His heart and mind, oblivious to the miles in his aging legs, still yearned for competition and for the simple joy of running. He was still able to glide over turf courses across the country with those same graceful strides, barely ruffling the blades of grass. In his eyes, the finish line still loomed large, and his unwavering determination to get there first was as strong as ever. He didn't know his age. All he knew was that this was what he was born for and what he still longed to do.

After all, it had been a long, hard road to the top. He had become the first nine-year-old Horse of the Year in history. How many nine-year-olds can win six consecutive grass stakes at five different tracks, from California to Chicago to New York? Although John was primarily a grass horse, he still is the only horse in history to win the famed Santa Anita Handicap twice, and the only horse other than Triple Crown winner Affirmed to win the prestigious Santa Anita Handicap and Jockey Club Gold Cup. He also accomplished the rare feat of carrying as much as 130 pounds to victory in stakes on both grass and dirt, and is the only horse ever to be voted Horse of the Year in non-consecutive years. There, no doubt, was quite a remarkable engine packed into that fifteen-hand, two-inch frame.

From July 6, 1979, to November 13, 1982, John started thirty-five consecutive times without finishing worse than fourth. It took a disastrous trip to Japan to end the streak.

During his career, John Henry defeated seventeen champions or classic winners. To demonstrate just how

far he surpassed all that came before him, he was the first horse to earn $3 million, the first horse to earn $4 million, the first horse to earn $5 million, and the first horse to earn $6 million. Because of his incredible rise to success, John was featured on NBC's *Today* show and was named by *People* magazine as one of the twenty-five most intriguing "people" of 1984.

An outcast because of a hot temper and a defiance of authority, John Henry somehow was able to lift himself out of obscurity and into legend. From that ornery youngster emerged a seven-time Eclipse Award winner and holder of two Horse of the Year titles. He had taken on the persona of his blue-collared namesake, the "steel-drivin' man," John Henry. It seemed as if nothing could stop this horse of steel.

When asked how long John Henry would race, his owner, Sam Rubin, joked, "until his bar mitzvah," signifying thirteen years of age. But in the end, with his thirst for competition still insatiable, John was betrayed by a nagging tendon in his right foreleg.

And now, here he was contentedly nibbling on hay in the familiar surroundings of a Tex Sutton aircraft, oblivious to the void he was about to leave in so many lives.

The flight was full, and John had been the last horse to load, which meant he'd be the first to disembark. There to greet him would be hordes of media, officials, and the governor of Kentucky, Martha Layne Collins, as well as Sam Rubin and his wife, Dorothy. There was no doubt that a star was arriving in the Bluegrass. Several days of festivities were planned, including a black-tie dinner and the governor's offical welcome on Saturday, August 31, which was declared "John Henry Day" at the Horse Park.

The McAnallys had come well stocked, with four bushels of carrots, and during the flight they kept going back to visit with their hero. "I just had to keep going back to look at him," Debbie said. "That eye. He had the most incredible eye. We had such mixed feelings during the flight. We knew we were losing him, but we also knew he deserved the kind of life he was about to begin. He had earned the right to go to the Horse Park."

All McAnally kept thinking about was the "big, empty stall" that awaited them when they returned home.

On the afternoon of August 26, 1985, John Henry arrived in Kentucky, returning to his place of birth. Governor Collins gave John several welcome pats on

the nose as he stood near the plane checking out all the activity. John was then vanned to his new home. As the sun began to set, it was time for John to be turned out in his paddock, which would be home for the remainder of his life. His groom Jose Mercado led him to the middle of the paddock and slowly removed the shank, leaving the halter on. Ron and Debbie stood by the fence, admittedly in tears. As Mercado walked away, leaving John standing there alone in the middle of the paddock, the horse let out a loud whinny that, sixteen years later, still resounds throughout Ron McAnally's mind and heart.

"He let out a cry like you've never heard before," McAnally recalled. "It was like he was asking, 'Are you going to leave me here alone?' It was really a sad and trying moment."

"That really choked us up," Debbie said. "He cried out continuously. He had such a yearning for companionship, and he felt like we were deserting him."

McAnally's unique relationship with John Henry enabled him on occasion to know what the horse was thinking, and this was one of those occasions. He had recalled times in the past when he'd have to van a shipment of horses from one California track to another. These were horses that were scheduled to race early in the meet, and McAnally wanted them stabled at the track where they were going to run. But John Henry's races often were at the end of the meet, and he'd be left behind. Whenever he saw vanloads of horses leaving the barn, he'd become "unglued." McAnally realized that John felt as if he were being deserted, and he was forced in the future to keep all his horses at one track and ship for individual races.

Now, John *was* being deserted, and there was nothing McAnally could do, except ask to have a horse placed in an adjoining paddock that night so John could see that he was indeed going to have the companionship of other horses. Once this was done, John settled down and began to adapt to his new home.

Few, if any, horses in history touched more lives than John Henry. Like a bargain-basement sale item, he always seemed to be available at a dirt-cheap price. Someone was always willing to buy the product at those prices, but no one was willing to keep it for very long. On three occasions, he was sold to the same person, Hal Snowden Jr. John fell into the hands of Cajuns,

Kentucky hardboots, a Japanese bloodstock agent, and, finally, a Jewish bicycle salesman. He liked no one and tested the few who liked him.

But for reasons unknown, John Henry was the chosen one, seemingly guided through his tumultuous early years by some force that was determined to deliver him into immortality. It was destined that this mean-spirited gelding become one of the most beloved horses in racing history, an inductee into the Hall of Fame and the subject of poems, songs, and one very striking statue at Arlington Park, aptly titled "Against All Odds."

The story of John Henry is one that will touch people of all ages for generations to come. Now, whenever an owner looks at a cheap, unwanted horse, he can close his eyes and envision that bronze figure at Arlington Park desperately reaching for the finish line in the first Arlington Million. And just maybe it will give him hope that his will be the next chosen one destined to succeed "against all odds."

Steve Haskin
Hamilton Square, New Jersey, 2001

CHAPTER 1

Chance Of A Lifetime

In the early spring of 1975, Golden Chance Farm in Lexington, Kentucky, was only months away from capturing the Preakness Stakes with Master Derby. The breeding season was productive, with an overflow of foals being born, and the farm was flourishing despite the death the year before of owner Robert Lehmann.

With so many foals, no one paid much attention to Once Double's bay colt, which arrived on March 9. Unwilling to sell any of their mares, Fred Lehmann, who was now running the farm for his mother, Verna, decided that some of the forty-plus weanlings had to be culled and put up for sale.

"My father hated selling horses," Lehmann said. "He was always afraid the good one was going to get away. But, financially, we had no choice. We just had so many we couldn't afford to send them all to the racetrack and pay training bills on them."

So, that summer, Lehmann, veterinarian Dr. Gordon Layton, and farm manager Ed Caswell stood outside the barn and inspected all the weanlings, then decided on which ones would go. One of those chosen was Once Double's foal, a smallish, plain-looking colt that was back at the knees, a condition in which the leg appears to have a backward arc instead of a forward arc in the area around the knee. "On conformation alone, he was one we kicked out," Lehmann said.

It would not be the first time John Henry was "kicked out" by his owner.

In that spring of '75, Golden Chance was a rapidly growing establishment. Robert Lehmann, a millionaire by the time he was twenty-seven, had spent ten years building it up. Lehmann set up Golden Chance as a family-run corporation, headed by him and Verna, with their five children the sole stockholders. Lehmann's passion in life, in addition to big-game hunting, was building and creating. "If you can't build," he once said, "you might as well die."

It was that philosophy that tempered his enthusiasm

over winning the 1970 Kentucky Derby with the $6,500 yearling purchase Dust Commander. Lehmann felt that because he did not arrange the mating of the sire and dam he had not created anything, and therefore did not earn the right to rejoice over the victory. Because of his lack of enthusiasm following the race, and his comment that winning the Derby was not as exciting as bagging a big-game animal, he was vilified by the media.

Lehmann, who had been ill with leukemia, knew he was dying, yet still continued to build. He expanded Golden Chance, and also built a bank, office building, motel, and restaurant in Clearwater, Florida. In the front yard of his house at Golden Chance, he constructed a 150-foot tower made of concrete slabs and a mausoleum that included the entrance doors from the old Metropolitan Opera House, gold-veined marble from Mexico, and Balmoral Red granite crypt covers from the same quarry in Finland that provided the crypt cover for Napoleon's tomb.

Lehmann died in the winter of 1974. Little did he realize that he was about to create another work of art, one that wouldn't come into the world until the following spring. The blueprint for this masterpiece, as unlikely as it seemed, was the mating of the Golden Chance stallion Ole Bob Bowers with the farm's home-bred mare Once Double.

Golden Chance stood Ole Bob Bowers for only a $500 stud fee and considered him as merely a clean-up stallion. The farm was thriving, housing some sixty mares. With only one stallion on the farm, Noblesse Oblige II, and another to come, Honey Jay, the Lehmanns couldn't afford to pay the stud fees required to breed to so many mares, so they went out and bought Ole Bob Bowers to breed to some of the leftovers.

Ole Bob Bowers was not exactly a hack, being by Hollywood Gold Cup winner Prince Blessed and inbred to Blue Larkspur, a descendant of the popular Domino line. Ole Bob Bowers won six of thirty career starts, including the Tanforan Handicap, in which he equaled the world record for a mile and an eighth. He hadn't done much at stud, however, siring only a few minor stakes winners.

Once Double, a large, big-boned mare, was by champion broodmare sire Double Jay, who also traced to Domino, but neither she nor her dam and granddam had produced a stakes winner. However, John Henry's fourth dam, Dustemall, won the prestigious Matron Stakes and produced 1935 Hopeful Stakes winner Red Rain. Dustemall's half sister, Fly Swatter, produced champion two-year-old filly First Flight, who was also voted overall two-year-old champion.

Golden Chance had an abundance of petite mares with a good deal of sprinting blood, and the Lehmanns were looking for something more robust to breed to Ole Bob Bowers in the hope of getting a big, strong distance horse. They also wanted more of an outcross — a less closely related horse — and this mating seemed to fit the bill. But more important, as Fred Lehmann said, "He was free."

Ole Bob Bowers had a bad reputation. He was extremely difficult to handle, especially going to the breeding shed. He had attacked several people on the farm, including Fred Lehmann's brother-in-law, whose arm he grabbed, ripping his watch off. Despite his cheap stud fee, no one in Kentucky had any interest in sending mares to him. His days at Golden Chance were numbered, and the year after John Henry was born, he was consigned to the Keeneland November breeding stock sale. There he was sold to Charles and Theora Crommer, who owned Beechwind Farms near Osseo, Michigan, for a mere $900.

"We were prepared to spend $5,000," Theora Crommer said in the *Horseman's Journal*. "We made one bid, and no one else did. The place went silent. I think they all laughed at us when we left the pavilion."

Also in 1976, Once Double was sold to Tommy Stevens, owner of Stevens Point Farm in Paris, Kentucky. Originally scheduled to go through the sales ring, Once Double was sold privately to Stevens for $5,000. As John Henry was emerging as a star in 1980, Stevens sold half-interest in her to John Gaines for $275,000. Once Double went on to produce two minor stakes horses, Looigloo and Double Dial. She then began to have problems carrying a foal to full term and eventually wound up producing a Quarter Horse foal when the embryo was transferred to another mare.

Back in the spring of 1975, John Henry wasn't making much of an impression, except for his temper.

Not only was he physically incorrect, he wasn't even the big, sturdy colt his breeders had hoped for. If he did get one thing from his sire, it was his ornery disposition. Bobby Paul, who was in charge of the foals and weanlings at the time, had little recollection of the colt's early days other than he was a "mean, studdish little bugger."

Paul certainly could understand the decision to get rid of him. "I remember we had a flock of foals that year," he recalled. "Mrs. Lehmann was shocked. That old mare had never produced anything, and her colt was real tough. He was just like his daddy, running around biting and kicking. The other horses acted like they were afraid, and they kept away from him. He jumped around and kicked even when we were leading him to the sale."

The colt just had too many things going against him. Mrs. Lehmann recalled that three veterinarians advised getting rid of him. They would not be the last veterinarians to give thumbs down to John Henry.

Nine soon-to-be yearlings, including the Ole Bob Bowers colt, were entered in the Keeneland January

mixed sale, known as Kentucky's "fire sale." In the pavilion was John Callaway, a breeder and trainer who owned a horse farm with his wife, Jean, in a rural area of Pee Wee Valley, about ten miles outside of Louisville. The Callaways had begun racing mainly at old Miles Park in Louisville and occasionally raced at Churchill Downs and Ellis Park in the summer. Training for Charles and Joanne Carraway, Callaway had a nice colt named Haut Brion, who had a tough time beating this one horse.

"The horse was from the family of Double Jay," Jean Callaway recalled. "After that summer was over, and we were constantly getting whipped by this colt, we went to the Keeneland January sale. John saw this little yearling colt, who was out of a Double Jay mare. We had no clue who Ole Bob Bowers was. It wasn't until later that we found out he was a real rogue and had almost killed somebody at the farm. When this little colt came out in the ring, he was scroungy as the dickens. He'd been hitting his head on the screen of his stall, and his head was all bloody. He looked pitiful."

John Callaway said he looked like a "drowned rat

with blood running off his forehead. He was a real mess."

But Callaway still liked the pedigree and decided to test the waters. When the auctioneer opened the bidding at $1,000, Callaway nudged it up to $1,100 and that was it. The colt was his. Of all the Golden Chance yearlings to sell, he was the cheapest. "With his pedigree, and what he looked like, $1,100 was a fair price," Fred Lehmann said.

The Callaways took the colt home and made the mistake of having a veterinarian look at him. "Oh my gosh," the vet said. "You might as well get rid of that one. He'll never make it."

As the colt grew, his knee deformity became more pronounced, and the vet, who Jean Callaway said shall remain nameless, again suggested they stop wasting their time. Feeling he wouldn't stand training, Callaway never even put a saddle on him. It also didn't take Callaway long to discover the colt's erratic and nasty disposition. In describing him, he used words like retarded, crazy, and weird. The colt usually took out his anger on his water buckets and feed tubs, ripping them off the wall and stomping on them.

But the Callaways did notice something else in the colt, and Jean admits that being relatively new to the business, they weren't able to fully comprehend it. They would stand by the fence of the large paddock and watch the colt scamper about with the other yearlings. All they said to each other was, "You know, he runs different from the others."

"When he ran across that field, he looked like he was diving into a pool of water," Jean Callaway recalled. "He just stretched out and glided over the ground with the most beautiful action. But at the time we didn't know that we were looking at anything special. An experienced eye would have caught that right off the bat, but we missed it. It wasn't until we discussed it a few years later that we realized what we were seeing back then."

There weren't any places for the Callaways to sell the colt, and if they were going to heed their vet's advice, they'd have to wait until the next Keeneland January mixed sale. Meanwhile, the horse needed a name. John Callaway, according to his wife, would name many of their horses with the first name John. He submitted five names for Ole Bob Bowers' son, including John Henry, the name immortalized in a song about a "steel-drivin' man." That was the one chosen.

Like the other yearlings, John Henry was broken in September and then turned out for the remainder of the winter. Training would have started when he turned two, but John was already destined for another trip to the sales ring. The Callaways had a large run-in barn and let the horses run free as much as possible. They would only put them up if the weather became unbearably cold. As long as John Henry was out running in the field, he was a "pussy cat," according to Jean Callaway. Considering he was never confined to a stall, the Callaways really had no idea that a panther lurked inside the pussycat. When the blacksmith came, Jean Callaway would hold John Henry, and the colt would just stand quietly, playing with the shank, while holding his foot up.

Then came the night before the sale. For a year, John Henry had been a free spirit, frolicking about in the field, content with the world. Now, he found himself back in the dreaded stall, being groomed and cleaned for his date with the auctioneer. Jean went in to feed him and John reared up like a wild horse. She dropped

the feed bucket and dashed out of the stall. "I think I lost ten years of my life right there," she said. "I didn't want to see him again. That was my last encounter with him. My final image of John Henry was up on his back legs. When my husband put him on the trailer and hauled him off, I said, 'Good riddance.' "

John Henry was off to the next phase of what was to be a tumultuous childhood, for him and those around him. For Golden Chance Farm, there were more glory days ahead, although one of their best horses, Run Dusty Run, had the misfortune of coming along the same year as Seattle Slew, and they had to settle for seconds in the Kentucky Derby and Belmont Stakes and third in the Preakness. Bad luck continued when Run Dusty Run finished first in the Travers Stakes, only to be disqualified. The Lehmanns sold Golden Chance in 1989. Some of the brothers and sisters wanted to go their separate ways, and the others couldn't afford to buy them out. Fred Lehmann still owns a couple of mares in Ohio.

The Callaways, who have since divorced, with Jean remaining in Kentucky and John heading to Florida, couldn't believe the fate that awaited their crooked, crazy little horse. When John Henry won the San Juan Capistrano three years later and had his picture on the cover of *The Blood-Horse*, Jean could only shake her head and say, "Can you believe it, our scroungy little horse that nobody wanted is on the cover of *The Blood-Horse*?"

As John Callaway said, "I made the best buy and the worst sale in the history of the Keeneland horse sale."

But there have been no regrets. Jean Callaway realizes that John Henry was a horse of destiny and had he remained with them, that destiny never would have been fulfilled. "If we had kept the horse, he probably would have stepped in a hole at Ellis Park and ruined one of those bad knees. And no one would have ever heard of him," she said. "It was just fate that brought John Henry and Ron McAnally together. He was able to take that talent and make something out of it."

Years later, Jean Callaway ran into McAnally and told him if it weren't for him, no one would have heard of John Henry. "He was the brains behind the success of that horse," she said. "He did everything right."

She had to ask him one question though. For years, she longed for the answer. "Just how did you turn this horse around?" she asked.

Without hesitation, McAnally replied, "I taught him to trust me."

CHAPTER 2

Doesn't Anyone Want This Horse?

I t was January 1977. The mighty Forego had just completed an amazing Horse of the Year campaign at the age of six, in which he emblazoned his name in the history books with a victory in the Marlboro Cup that will be talked about for generations to come. Another Eclipse Award-winning year was to follow for the great gelding before his retirement in July of 1978.

The racing world also eagerly awaited the three-year-old campaign of the brilliant Seattle Slew, champion two-year-old of 1976. With the memory of Secretariat's titanic feats still fresh after three years, and with superstars Affirmed and Alydar and Spectacular Bid on the near horizon, it was truly a time for greatness.

Light years from this world of superheroes was the Keeneland January mixed sale. Here, there were no thoughts of Secretariat or Forego. At this sale, a smattering of Kentucky hardboots gathered to look for bargains. These were horsemen basically looking for action, and, most important, a means of survival.

Attending the 1977 sale was Harold "Bubba" Snowden Jr., who was managing his father's Fairfield Farm north of Lexington. The Snowdens were well respected for their ability to pick out good horses. Little did Bubba realize that of all the horses catalogued for the sale, one would become a major part of his life for the next two and a half years. He, of course, had no way of knowing that during that time he would be helping to mold a horse who would one day continue the legacy of greatness left by the superstars of the seventies.

A blizzard just prior to the sale prevented many out-of-state horses from getting to Lexington, and as a result far fewer horses were sold than catalogued. Of the 512 that did sell, one that caught Snowden's eye was hip number 570, a still unbroken two-year-old named John Henry. Snowden actually liked his sire, Ole Bob Bowers. He recalled several of the stallion's offspring that had performed well at Keeneland the year before.

Snowden even overlooked the colt's knees. He

thought to himself, "Golly, I'll just buy this horse, break him, and sell him privately during the Keeneland meet."

Once again, there was little interest in the colt, and Snowden was able to get him for $2,200. Although well below the sale average of just over $9,000, it still was a 100-percent profit for the Callaways. John Henry was off to his third home, and despite going through the sales ring twice, he still was virtually valueless.

Snowden's first impressions of John Henry were no different than anyone else's. "He was a dumpy little horse and back at the knees," he said. "He was ugly, and there really wasn't anything to him at all other than he had a nice foot on him. That was it."

But that wasn't it. There was more to John Henry, and it didn't take Snowden long to discover the colt's dirty little secret. For the first few days, Snowden let John relax and get used to his new environment. But he soon discovered John was a terror in the stall. He had no trouble breaking the horse, but, unfortunately, that winter was one of the worst in memory, with several feet of snow and frigid temperatures. That meant the horses had to spend more time than normal in their stalls. John went through feed tubs and water buckets on a regular basis. Not only would he destroy the feed tubs, he'd rip the screws out of the wall.

"All of a sudden, this little sonofagun is a monster," Snowden said. "Outside the stall, he was very professional and was no problem training. But he was just a bastard in his stall."

Snowden took John Henry to Keeneland in late February and jogged him in the shedrow, because the snow was too deep to bring him to the track. With snow still on the ground in March and temperatures in the twenties, John Henry remained stuck in his stall and continued to wreak havoc. One day, Snowden told his vet, Jim Boucher, "Let's cut this horse." But the vet said it was too cold to castrate him, as he would need to be exercised afterward. Snowden had been feeding John by putting the feed tub on the floor of his stall rather than hooking it up to the screw-outs, which he'd only rip out of the wall anyway. John would still put his foot through the plastic feed tubs, which had to be replaced regularly. Eventually, the temperature warmed up to the low forties, and John Henry was gelded.

In mid-April, Snowden found a buyer for the horse. Akiko McVarish, a Japanese-born bloodstock agent who had moved to the United States and married an Irishman, had been doing business with Snowden while boarding some horses at his farm. John Henry had begun to show some promise and was about forty days from running. Snowden told McVarish, "Akiko, I've got this horse who can run a little bit. You ought to buy him. He's sound as a bell of brass, and you should make some money with him."

McVarish came to the barn to look at the horse. Her veterinarian, Dr. Warren Perez, was in Japan at the time, so McVarish made Snowden an unusual offer. "She told me, 'I'll give you $7,500 for him and pay the training bill. When Warren gets back, I'll have him look at the horse. If he doesn't like him, you give me the money back,' " Snowden recalled. "I didn't have anyone else who was interested, so I took the deal. She left the horse with me, and then, a month later, Dr. Perez got back from Japan. He examined the horse and said, 'This horse will never stand training. Akiko, you need to get your money back.' She called me up and apologized. I refunded her money, and now I got this horse back again."

But it wouldn't be for long. The following month at

Keeneland, Snowden was visited by two women from Louisiana, Colleen Madere from New Orleans and Dorthea Lingo from Baton Rouge. They told Snowden they had been looking for a horse over at the Murty brothers' farm, and the Murtys suggested they come see him. Snowden could see immediately that the feisty, outspoken Madere was the one he'd have to deal with.

When he asked what he could do for them, Madere said, "I'm looking to buy a horse, baby."

"What kind of horse do you want?" Snowden asked.

"One that's gonna win," she answered.

She told Snowden she had between $10,000 and $15,000 to spend, and that the cheapest thing the Murtys had was $30,000. When he asked if they had raced horses before, she said they had, with trainer Anatole Bourque, but they had brought along their new trainer, Phil Marino, who was up at the track kitchen. The year before, Marino had won a couple of small stakes for Madere with a horse named My Mito. They decided to take the winnings and go to Kentucky to buy a horse or two.

Madere had been involved in rooster fighting and

other unusual endeavors, and Snowden could tell she had plenty of street smarts. "She was quite a character," he said. "She was dressed like she had money, with high heels and a fancy hat, and I'll bet she had a feather in her hat for every rooster she fought." After she introduced Snowden to Marino, they decided to let the trainer take the horse out to the track and breeze him.

Marino went to the barn to get John Henry, and the first thing he noticed when he approached his stall was a fifty-five-gallon drum of molasses shoved up against the front of the Dutch doors. "There was all this banging and screaming going on in the stall," he said. "I said to myself, 'What the hell did I get myself into.'"

Just then, John Henry's groom, an old-timer named Quince Parker, came out of the stall and told Marino, "Don't worry about him, son. He'll be all right once I get the bridle on him." It took Parker about ten minutes to catch the horse, but once he did and put the bridle on, John quieted down and behaved beautifully. The first time around the track, however, John acted greenly, bouncing off the rail a few times. The second time around was a different story.

"I finally got him straightened out where I could

smooch to him, and when I did, he took off and got low to the ground on me in about four jumps," Marino said. "I had sat on a lot of top horses and some champions and I knew class when I saw it. And this colt had a lot of class."

When price was discussed, Snowden asked for $10,000, but Marino felt it was too high, and the three of them left. The following day, Marino asked Snowden what he'd take for the horse. Snowden then contacted Madere and said he had another two-year-old and he'd sell her both horses for $11,000. Marino returned to look at the other colt and gave the okay.

Madere had one stipulation. She told Snowden, "Baby, I'll give you the $11,000, but I'll tell you what I want you to do. I want you to get (John Henry) ready to run and okayed out of the gate, and then ship him to Jefferson Downs. And I don't want anyone screwing it up."

When John Henry was one work away from running, Snowden called Madere and told her the horse had been okayed from the gate and was just about ready to run. "Okay, baby," she said. "You ship him down here and I'll call Phil. Send me a bill."

So, Bubba Snowden finally bid farewell to John Henry...for now.

JOHN HENRY

CHAPTER 3

Cajun Days

For the first two years of his life, John Henry had been peddled like a cheap wristwatch. All the polishing couldn't hide the fact that he was liable to stop ticking at any time. Sure, his stride and professionalism led some to believe that maybe there was a fine piece of machinery beneath the surface. But the bottom line was the colt had a mediocre pedigree, was not much to look at, had a major flaw in conformation, and was a savage in his stall. His legs had been used more as weapons than as instruments of speed.

But if John had one positive trait, it was his ability to touch people's lives. And regardless of his early misadventures, none of his owners ever lost money with him. Of course, everyone knows how John affected the lives of Ron McAnally and Sam Rubin, but no one's life was affected more by the horse than Phil Marino's.

Following the sale of John Henry, Marino, like everyone before him, discovered the keg of dynamite that had just been delivered to his barn. Marino had aluminum feed buckets, and in the first week alone, John put his feet through seven of them after he finished eating. Marino replaced them with plastic tubs and, like Snowden, just left them on the floor of the stall. The good news was that John didn't tear them up. The bad news was that the stalls only had partial partitions, and when Marino arrived each morning, John's feed tub was three or four stalls down the shedrow in another horse's stall. He had managed to grab it and fling it over the partition. Marino eventually gave John a soccer ball to play with, and he would squat down on his knees and bat it around. Then, once he was finished with it, he'd kick it out of the stall.

But Marino also discovered that once he put the bridle on John, Mr. Hyde quickly turned into Dr. Jekyll. "He was a pussycat," Marino said. "He was such a ham it would take me forty-five minutes to get him to the track. He'd just stand there and look around. And on the way home, he'd stop and graze along the way."

Because John was so "nutty" and constantly getting

into trouble, Marino nicknamed him "Squirrel." Although John behaved once the bridle was on, getting it on could be quite an adventure. Unlike most trainers who used rubber tie chains, Marino's were chain link, the kind you'd use to tie up a bicycle. He would double it and hook it to the wall, and John still would try to rear. "He'd get up and try to jump on top of you and paw and kick you," he said. "And he'd bite you while you were doing him up. But he never hurt anyone. He was very calculated about everything he did. He just wanted to let you know who was the boss."

When Marino started breezing John Henry, he knew he had a runner on his hands. In between works, whenever they got to the top of the stretch, Marino would let him gallop out strong to the wire. Soon, an outrider had to come pick them up. John had learned that when he came to the head of the stretch, it was time to run. The first time Marino worked him from the gate, he broke with a promising two-year-old, trained by Sal Tassistro, who had already won for $50,000. The two hooked up at the break and John beat Tassistro's horse, blazing the three-eighths in :34 flat. And Marino never even asked John to run.

Marino had been so impressed with John Henry he told Colleen Madere, "I'm gonna win the Lafayette Futurity with this horse."

"She thought I was crazy," Marino said. "So did everyone else. I kept braggin' on him all the time, and they all thought I was nuts saying that about a horse who hadn't even raced."

Finally, on May 20, 1977, John Henry was ready to become a racehorse. Once those gates opened to launch his career, all his nefarious deeds would be put behind him. Marino, who had only four stalls, was stabled in the same barn as Bernie Flint. Even though Flint had thirty horses and was among the leading trainers at the meet, purses were negligible, and both he and Marino were struggling to eke out an existence.

Flint also had a horse, named You Sexy Thing, in the race, a four-furlong maiden special weight event at Jefferson Downs. "Bernie bet the last fifty dollars he had in his pocket on his horse," Marino said.

"Those were rough days," Flint added. "With maiden purses only $2,800, you had to bet your horses and just go out there and work hard every day. Phil was just starting out and doing most of the work by himself. Jefferson Downs was the last place you'd expect to find a future champion. I remember John Henry as this gangly thing who was mean as hell."

With Marino's bragging and the horse's fast works, John Henry was sent off as the 17-10 second choice. John broke a bit slowly from the rail and settled into fifth. At the eighth pole, he still was four lengths off the lead and appeared beaten. But under the hard driving of jockey Glen Spiehler, John showed the courage and tenacity that would become his trademark and just got up at the wire to nose out You Sexy Thing.

"After that race, we knew we had a nice horse on our hands," said Marino. "Mrs. Madere was happy, because she also bet quite a lot of money on him. But the atmosphere in the winner's circle was more professional than anything else."

John ran well in his next two starts in allowance company, but could only manage a second and a third. Then, on July 29, he was entered in a six-furlong handicap. On the far turn, a horse went down in front of John, who was unable to avoid the fallen horse and toppled over him. Miraculously, John wasn't hurt.

Soon after, Marino put him in another overnight

handicap, and it began to look as if John's misfortunes were carrying over onto the racetrack. Shortly after the break, all the lights went out, and there was chaos on the track, as horses and jockeys scrambled about aimlessly in the dark. "Oh, God," Marino said from his box. "He's ruined. He's gonna get hurt."

When the lights came back on, three jockeys were injured, and two horses had run through the gap, one jumping into the nearby canal and the other running loose in the barn area. And there was John Henry standing at the seven-eighths pole with the rider on his back. "It looked like he was standing there posing for pictures," Marino said. "He never turned a hair."

The race was ruled no contest. After winning an allowance race by three lengths, John was entered in a trial for the Lafayette Futurity, the race that Marino predicted months earlier John Henry would win.

In the paddock, Madere told Marino, "Just qualify with him. I'm very superstitious about going into a big race off a win."

"I told her, 'You tell the jock that. I'm in here to win it,'" Marino said. "When he finished second (in the trial) and still had the second-fastest qualifying time, I knew I was a cinch to win the Futurity."

For the next ten days, Marino slept on a cot in front of John's stall to keep an eye on him. John still managed to rip his eye, just above the eyelash, but it was nothing serious. That year, the winner's purse for the six-furlong Futurity was a record $43,225, a fortune for a trainer at Evangeline Downs.

The morning of the race, Marino snuck out on the track at 4:30 and blew John out an eighth of a mile. "It was the fastest eighth I'd ever gone on a horse," he said. "I knew right then and there he was gonna win."

John was sent off at 5-1 and broke from the rail in the twelve-horse field. The track had come up sloppy due to a driving rain storm, and jockey Alonzo Guajardo was able to settle him in fourth, five lengths off the lead. At the eighth pole, he still had two and a half lengths to make up. Like in his debut, John dug down and gave it everything. With hurricane-force winds and heavy rain blowing in his face, he closed relentlessly, just getting up to win by a head over Lil' Liza Jayne.

"That night we were flying high," Marino said. "We all went out to dinner and Mrs. Madere ordered a case of champagne."

Marino felt like he was on top of the world. John Henry had come through for him, and everything seemed right with the world. But then the stable moved to Fair Grounds, and that's when, as Marino said, "All hell broke loose."

John Henry completely lost his form. On the surface it looked as if he simply couldn't handle the jump in class from Evangeline and Jefferson. Marino and Madere began to argue constantly. Marino tried to tell her John just couldn't handle the track.

"The first time I ran him, in the Hospitality Stakes, he finished fifth and came back like he had run forty miles," Marino said. "And I knew he was fit."

Marino told Madere, "Either there's something wrong with him or he just doesn't like the racetrack." One bad race after another followed. Marino called noted Kentucky veterinarian Dr. Alex Harthill to come look at John and had blacksmith Jack Reynolds put new shoes on him.

"Everyone said there's nothing wrong with him," Marino said. "They all concluded it was the racetrack. I kept trying to relay that to Mrs. Madere, but she didn't want to hear any of it."

John Henry had now turned three, and Marino decided to stretch him out to two turns, hoping that would help turn him around. It didn't, as John threw in two more dull performances. After one of the races, he returned to the barn and was given a bath. Marino started walking him, and before he knew it, his jacket sleeve was in John's mouth. John picked Marino up off the ground and took off down the shedrow, dragging him along. Marino was being lifted in the air and was completely helpless.

Fortunately, Mike Petrie, a trainer who shared Marino's barn, grabbed John and was able to stop him, as John finally let go of his trainer. "Thank God I had a goose down jacket or he would have taken a big chunk out of me," Marino said. "That's how mad the horse was. You could tell something was bothering him. He simply was pissed. I kept relaying this to Mrs. Madere."

Marino tried everything. Blinkers didn't work, nor did dropping him into claiming races. Twice John ran for a $25,000 tag, and once for $20,000. The best he could do was a third-place finish. Since his victory in the Lafayette Futurity, John Henry had run nine times, finishing out of the money in seven of them. It was now late March of his three-year-old year, and the

horse's future looked bleak. It seemed a return to the bush tracks was all that awaited him. Had John Henry's demons finally sealed his fate?

Madere's patience was wearing thin. In early April, Marino had made arrangements with a friend, trainer James Navarre, to send John Henry to Oaklawn Park, where he'd have a stall for him. At five in the morning, the van was outside the barn at Fair Grounds, with all the tack loaded. Fifteen minutes later, Marino received a call from Madere telling him to cancel the trip.

"She owned a poodle parlor, grooming dogs," he said, "and she told me they had too many dogs to groom, and that she couldn't make the trip. I said to her, 'Mrs. Madere, I'm twenty-seven years old. I think I'm qualified to follow a van 350 miles up the road. She said, 'Where he goes, I go, or he don't go at all.' "

Marino had had enough. He told Madere that the van was loaded and ready to go somewhere. "I'm not running him at Fair Grounds again," Marino said. "So, if he's not going to Oaklawn, then van him up to Keeneland and sell him."

That was the end of Marino's relationship with Madere, as the two decided to part. John Henry had no trainer and no place to go, so Madere turned to the only person who could help. Instead of going to Oaklawn, John wound up heading back to Keeneland, to none other than Bubba Snowden.

Madere had called Snowden and told him they couldn't do any good with John Henry and asked if he could sell him...again. She told him that the vets couldn't find anything wrong with him. "I don't want to send him to anyone but you," she said, "because you know his disposition."

So, John Henry returned to Snowden, who took X-rays of the horse's knees and ankles. He was perfectly sound, and Snowden asked Madere what she wanted for him. She said $25,000, but he told her it would be very difficult to sell a horse for that price when he had just been beaten for that amount, and finished up the track running for $20,000. She told him to try, but no one was interested. Snowden then offered a swap. He would take John Henry in exchange for a couple of two-year-olds — a colt and a filly. Madere agreed and John Henry belonged to Snowden for the third time.

For Phil Marino, the John Henry saga was far from over. The horse he had trained, groomed, exercised,

and slept with would become a national hero, earning millions of dollars, while he was forced to come to terms with his lowly existence. The more successful the horse became, the deeper Marino would sink, until he hit rock bottom.

"It ruined me," he said. "It was like they pulled the plug on me. I really didn't care about anything and started drinking and doing drugs. I had a few horses, but every morning I'd get up and look out my tack-room door, and I'd see nothing but $2,000 claimers looking back at me, while this horse is out there winning $500,000 stakes every few weeks."

Marino's days at Evangeline Downs, in particular, were a nightmare. He was stabled there when John Henry won his two Arlington Millions. After each race, the same announcement was made over the loudspeaker: "Phil Marino, John Henry just won another million. How are you feeling today?"

"Whenever I'd try to hustle clients, I'd get the same thing: 'Oh, you couldn't win with John Henry. How are you going to win with my horse?' " Marino said.

Marino couldn't take it any longer. Life as a Thoroughbred trainer had turned into a living hell, and he descended deeper into drugs and alcohol. He drank a fifth of vodka a day and had to support a $2,400-a-week cocaine habit.

"This went on through all the years John Henry raced," Marino said. "I was labeled as the man who couldn't win with John Henry. Every time he ran, I crawled deeper and deeper into my hole, and I really didn't care if I lived or died."

Then came the day in 1985 that changed Marino's life completely. It was just another hot July morning, with another empty day awaiting him. He was at the home of his jockey, and the two had gotten drunk the night before. When Marino awoke the next morning, he found the rider passed out on the floor. He turned on the radio, and remembers it was exactly 7:38 when he heard the news of John Henry's retirement.

"I pushed the vodka and cocaine away, and I haven't had a drink or taken a drug since," he said. "It was like a veil had been lifted off my head."

Through his ordeal Marino never stopped caring about John Henry. "We always had a special relationship," he said. "And we still do. I visit him at the Horse Park at least six or seven times when we're stabled in

Kentucky. He still comes running over to me when I call him Squirrel. We had a game we played when he wasn't trying to kill me. I'd take the palm of my hand and he'd open his mouth where just his teeth were showing. I'd push the palm of my hand against his mouth and we'd play like a tug-o-war back and forth. And we still do to this day. Every time I go see him, I pull off a little piece of his tail and give it to one of my friends. And I always give the girls there some money to make sure he has enough carrots. Even after all these years, and all I went through, whenever I visit old John, he still brings tears to my eyes."

Marino built up a successful stable, with the support of owner Sandi Kleemann, and leased a farm in Kentucky. "I was blessed when Sandi Kleemann came into my life as an owner," he said. "Mrs. Madere never called or stayed in touch with me. I heard she passed away a couple of years after we lost the horse. The Good Lord put me to the test. He taught me humility and made me a better person. He took me from the lowest depths to the top of the world."

JOHN HENRY

CHAPTER 4

"What color is a gelding?"

Imagine buying stock in C-T-R (Computing-Tabulating-Recording Co.) on three separate occasions in the early 1920s, finally selling it, then watching the company evolve into IBM. That's pretty much what happened to Bubba Snowden, who had no way of knowing the cheap stock named John Henry he was wheeling and dealing for so long was going to become IBM.

But in the reality of Thoroughbred racing, owning hidden treasure does not often lead to wealth. Some believe higher forces guided John Henry to his destiny and Snowden simply was not part of the master plan.

All Snowden knew when he got John Henry back was that it was the beginning of April, the 1978 racing season was in full swing, and he needed to sell his old friend again. When he breezed the horse at Keeneland, John sizzled five furlongs in :59 flat, justifying Marino's belief that the horse needed to get away from Fair Grounds.

John's recent form was dismal, but the gelding still had won a futurity, even if it was at Evangeline Downs, and had earned more than $50,000. Snowden went shopping for potential buyers, but none could be found.

"He was pretty damn hard to sell," Snowden recalled. "Finally, I said, 'Golly, I've got to run this sonofabitch to re-establish his value.' "

On April 11, Snowden ran John Henry in a six-furlong allowance race at Keeneland, and he finished an even fourth, beaten nine and a half lengths, at 6-1. What was encouraging was that the race was run in a snappy 1:09 3/5.

"I knew John wasn't going to win this race," Snowden said. "The winner was a horse called Johnny Blade, who I had broken with John Henry, and there was no way John was going to beat this horse. But all I wanted was to get his value up where I could ask for $25,000. That's what Colleen wanted, so I thought I'd go for that figure, too."

Snowden not only was actively trying to sell John Henry locally, he let the word get out wherever he could. He worked John again after the Keeneland race and decided to point him for a race at Churchill Downs. Meanwhile, events were taking place in New York that would ultimately, and dramatically, change the lives of several people...and one racehorse.

Sam Rubin was sixty-three years old, and his experience with horses had been restricted to betting on them and racing one through the streets of the Bronx, New York, in his youth. That horse, however, was pulling a laundry wagon at the time. Rubin was a tough kid, but he had to be growing up on New York's Lower East Side and the Bronx. Rubin would steal fruit and vegetables off the corner stand and coal off the trucks. He gambled on anything and smoked three packs of cigarettes a day.

Rubin's parents had fled Czarist Russia and settled in Manhattan. His father died when Sam was very young, and his mother moved him and his three older siblings to the Bronx. To support his family, Sam delivered groceries and sold newspapers on the subway. He even sold banners and souvenirs at Yankee Stadium, and often was robbed and beaten. Rubin quit high school to become a "wolf" on Wall Street after seeing the movie, "Wolf of Wall Street." When he discovered Wall Street didn't need any more wolves, he took a job driving a horse-drawn laundry wagon.

As soon as Rubin got up on the wagon, he was

transformed into Earl Sande, sitting atop a noble steed. Only his noble steed was a big, old bay horse named Clotch'y. Never one to pass up a friendly wager, Rubin would bet the drivers of the fruit wagon and ice wagon a buck that he could beat them once around the block. This wasn't exactly like running around Belmont Park, as they had to whiz by pushcarts and sidewalk stands, and avoid kids playing ball and other forms of traffic. Each afternoon, at the end of his route, he had to get off the wagon two blocks from the stable, because there was always someone from the American Society for the Prevention of Cruelty to Animals there waiting for him. "I was on the most-wanted list of the ASPCA," he said. "The horse would come back with his tongue hanging out, and they were waiting for me with base- ball bats to kill me. I actually was afraid of that horse. He was big and powerful, and when I wanted to go right and he wanted to go left, he usually got his way."

Rubin then got a job at the city hall post office, working the night shift. At three in the morning, he would go across the street to a restaurant for "lunch." The following day's *New York Daily Mirror* was already on the newsstands, and people would buy it and start handicapping the races. One night, he picked a horse and said to a bookie, "Okay, give me two dollars on him." The horse won and paid sixty-six dollars, and Rubin thought, "How long has this been going on?"

Now hooked on betting horses, he made $4,000 in one day at the old Empire City Racetrack and became an instant major player, no longer content with making small wagers. He left the post office and opened his own laundry. But he continued to bet above his means and soon found himself in debt to a bookmaker for $5,600 and unable to pay it. He borrowed $3,200 from his mother and sold his laundry for $2,400. The runner who took the money found out what Rubin had done to get it and told his boss. The bookie was so astounded he bought back his laundry for him, but never took another bet from him.

Married now, Rubin still didn't learn his lesson and became even more of a degenerate gambler, shooting craps and betting thousands on football games. He got rid of the laundry and began selling Howdy Doody puppets, eventually becoming a bicycle salesman. As he traveled around the country selling his bikes, his list of racetracks grew rapidly.

Then, just like that, he woke up one morning and

decided to give up gambling to concentrate on his bicycle business. There was enough competition importing bicycles to quench his appetite for action. Soon, he signed on to represent a major Japanese trading firm, C. Itoh and Company, and his business began to prosper. But just as things were going great, Lil, his wife of thirty-nine years, passed away.

A devastated Rubin discovered he was incapable of living alone. While returning to Manhattan from a business trip to Asia, he began thinking about an old friend, Dorothy Levinson, whom he hadn't seen in thirty years. He thought of the good times he and Lil used to have when they double dated with Dorothy and her husband. Rubin found out that Dorothy had been widowed for four years and was living in Coral Gables, Florida. He hopped on a plane and immediately called her after arriving. They met in the lobby of the Doral Beach Hotel in Miami and shared a tearful reunion. As they hugged and kissed, people in the lobby began applauding. Six months later they were married.

One day in late April of 1978, Rubin came home from the office early and had an inspiration. "Out of the blue, I told Dorothy, 'I'm going to take $150,000 and buy two racehorses, one for $50,000 and one for $25,000, and use the rest for expenses,'" Rubin recalled. "I just wanted to have some fun and some action, and when it was over, it was over. Once I blew the money that would be the end of owning horses. What's she going to say? It was my money, so I decided to do it."

That same afternoon, the Rubins went to Aqueduct and saw Sam's friend Joe Taub eating lunch. Taub owned the New Jersey Nets basketball team and several quality horses, and that winter and spring he had enjoyed the heroics of his brilliant colt Sensitive Prince, winner of the Hutcheson and Fountain of Youth Stakes. Sensitive Prince would go into the Kentucky Derby unbeaten, but would tire after setting most of the pace against the likes of Affirmed and Alydar.

"Hey, Joe, you know anybody around who's got any $25,000 horses for sale or a good one for $50,000?" Rubin asked him.

"Not off hand, Sam. I don't fool around with cheap horses," said Taub, whose purchases were more in the $100,000 to $200,000 range.

The Rubins sat down to lunch, and several minutes later they were approached by agent Jimmy Ferraro.

"Mr. Rubin, Mrs. Rubin, Joe Taub says you're interested in buying a horse for $25,000," Ferraro said. "I happen to know of one in Kentucky. This guy Hal Snowden owns him, and he's got him up for sale."

Rubin said he was interested, and Ferraro arranged for him to meet trainer Bobby Donato, who only had three or four horses in training at the time. "Jimmy told me, 'Bobby, I might have an owner for you,' " Donato said. "He wants to get into the business, and I think you should go meet him."

Donato hooked up with Rubin, then called Snowden and arranged to come down and look at John Henry. Snowden had two other horses for sale as well. Donato flew to Lexington and brought a check for $25,000 from Rubin, made out to Snowden.

"I didn't know Bobby," Snowden said. "He told me he had a new client who's in the bicycle business, and he wanted to make sure he got him a good horse who can win and was ready to run. I told him we had just taken X-rays three weeks earlier and the horse was absolutely sound. I said the horse should like the slop, being by Ole Bob Bowers, and that he should also like the grass. He flew down and watched the horse jog, and said, 'He'll do.' "

"I didn't like the other two, but I did like John Henry," Donato said. "He was a little back in the knees, but only a hair. Certainly not enough to really make you notice it. Anyway, when you buy a horse for $25,000 who's been running, what do you want, perfect conformation on top of it? Guys spend over a million dollars for a horse and don't get perfect conformation."

The deal was made, and Snowden shipped John Henry to Donato in New York. Rubin through the years has told a different version of his purchase of John Henry. He said after meeting with Ferraro, he called Snowden and made the deal over the phone, telling Snowden to send the horse to New York. If he vetted out, Rubin would send him a check. Snowden and Donato both insist that's not the way it happened, that it was Donato who came down to Kentucky and made the deal. Neither has seen the other since, yet their accounts of the incident match up in every detail.

"Bobby flew in on USAir," Snowden said, "and I can remember exactly what he was wearing. First off, there is no way I would ever sell a horse and send him to New York to someone I never even heard of without getting paid first."

In any event, Sam Rubin had himself a racehorse. After the sale, one of his friends came over to him and said, "Sam, I hear you bought a horse the other day. What kind of horse did you buy?" Rubin thought for a second and realized he had no idea what he had bought. Shortly after, he ran into Jimmy Ferraro and he asked him, "Jimmy, what did I buy?"

"You bought a gelding," he replied.

"What color is that?" Rubin asked.

For Bubba Snowden, John Henry finally was out of his life for good. Like all the others who let the moonbeam slip out of their hands, Snowden was philosophical. "As someone who buys and sells horses," he said, "I learned a long time ago that I'd rather regret selling one than regret keeping one."

Years later, after John Henry had made his way into the history books, Snowden's brother-in-law, Bill North, gave him a photo of John with Bill Shoemaker aboard. At the bottom of the photo, he had written a caption to make it seem as if the horse were speaking. All it said was, "I tried to tell you."

CHAPTER 5

Greener Pastures

B obby Donato was not exactly a household name in New York. In 1977 his horses won twelve races from ninety starts and earned $108,050. Donato had made quite an unusual leap into the Sport of Kings, having served for seven years on the Philadelphia Police Department's vice squad. He was forced to give up active work after fracturing his kneecap in a chase. Rather than accept a desk job, he quit the force and pondered what to do with his life. He found his answer during a visit to Garden State Park, where he was introduced by a friend to trainer Joe Pierce Jr. Donato became friendly with Pierce, and eventually went to work for him and his father, serving as an assistant for three years.

In 1971 he passed his trainer's test and managed to pick up a few horses. One of them was an old cripple named Swistic, who hadn't run in six months. The first time Donato ran him he won and paid $49.80.

Now, here Donato was, seven years later, still looking for his first big break. When Donato brought John Henry to his new home in Barn 7 at Aqueduct, he knew nothing of the horse's wicked ways. All he was aware of was that he had just bought a three-year-old gelding for $25,000. He had done research on the horse before going down to Kentucky and believed he was worth the money and that his pedigree suggested he should like the grass.

Rubin also knew little about John Henry and had no idea that his new possession had already been rejected several times. "I was just in it for fun and for the thrill of actually owning a horse," he said. "I figured we'd run him and see what happens. If someone had told me what I was in for, I would have laughed in their face."

The first person to realize that the stable's newest resident had a personality problem was his groom Pablo "Junior" Cosme. "He was pretty wild, and he'd bite and kick all the time," Cosme recalled. "We had to put up a screen, because he'd bite everybody coming down the shed. He got me a couple of times, but mostly I ignored him."

Cosme tried to get to know John and have the horse get used to him. He had a Labrador retriever named Opie, who became good friends with John and would sleep in his stall, practically right up against him. John would nibble Opie a little and play with him, and that seemed to settle him.

Right from the start, John breezed impressively on the dirt, but when Donato started galloping him on the grass, he noticed the same thing the Callaways had several years earlier. The horse just seemed to glide over it. But, unlike the Callaways, he knew what he was looking at. He told Cosme, "Hey, Junior, I think we got a nice horse here. He really moves well on the turf."

Aqueduct was nearing the end of its meet, and Donato needed to find a race for John Henry. There was a $25,000 claiming race at six furlongs, and Donato figured no one was going to claim a horse who wasn't able to win for that price at Fair Grounds. And he had to run John Henry somewhere to get him ready for his first crack at the turf. But the horse had run a fairly decent race in allowance company at Keeneland, and it was risky to tempt fate when you had a horse who looked to have a future on the grass. In addition,

if John were claimed, Rubin's new adventure would be over before it even began.

On Sunday, May 21, John Henry made his first start in New York, racing in the name of Dotsam Stable, derived from the combining of the names Dorothy and Sam. The day before, the racing world had thrilled to another heart-pounding stretch duel between Affirmed and Alydar in the Preakness. With his dramatic neck victory, Affirmed was on the threshold of a Triple Crown sweep. If someone had said, that in addition to Affirmed and Alydar, another future Hall of Famer from the same crop would be running that weekend, you'd certainly be hard pressed to find him in the second half of the Aqueduct daily double — a $25,000 claiming race.

John Henry was sent off at 12-1 under Angel Santiago and drew off to win by two and a half lengths in 1:12 3/5. As John left the track, Donato told Rubin he thought the horse had a good grass foot. "I didn't know what he was talking about," Rubin said. "I never heard of a grass foot, so I'm looking for grass growing out of his foot."

"Sam won around $100,000 betting that race," Donato said. "I gave him the (daily) double cold, and told him to bet anything he wanted on John Henry."

After Belmont Park opened, Donato found a grass race for John Henry, a $35,000 claiming race going a mile and a sixteenth. Once again he was putting Rubin's new toy out there on a silver platter for any-one to snatch away from him. But this time Donato had more to worry about. John Henry was coming off a win, and for anyone willing to take the chance he'd make a good grass horse, the $10,000 jump in price did not seem like a lot.

On June 1, John Henry walked into stall number one in the starting gate and into history. The gates opened, and when John took that first step on this new, lush sur-face he discovered a fresh bounce to his step. He could barely feel his feet touch the ground. His legs were in perfect unison. He was going faster and faster. He was flying. The thunder of hooves pounding on dirt that he had been so used to was fading. There were no cracks of the whip; no jockeys shouting; just the sound of his own feet skimming over the blades of grass. He crossed the finish line fourteen lengths in front. And he didn't want it to end. He wanted to keep running, not realizing that a whole new world awaited him. Junior Cosme put it best: "After that race, he became John Henry."

But as Donato made his way down to the winner's circle, his elation was tempered by feelings of fear and uncertainty. He knew that the monster he had unleashed might be spending that night in someone else's barn. All he kept saying was, "God, I hope I didn't lose him."

The claim box again was empty. For the eighth time in John Henry's young life, someone had blown an opportunity to own a super horse.

"Needless to say, John Henry never saw a claiming race again," Donato said.

John then moved up in class to allowance company and just got up to beat a good horse named Turn of Coin by a neck, covering the mile and a sixteenth in a swift 1:41 1/5. With John Henry an obvious bargain purchase, Rubin decided to return to the well and try to pull up more of this magical elixir. He and Snowden negotiated a deal whereby Rubin purchased two more horses. But he never told Donato about it, and when his trainer found out which two horses he had purchased, he couldn't believe it. He knew both horses very well and immediately called Rubin.

"Sam, those are the two horses I turned down in

Kentucky," Donato said. "Why would you buy them?"

Rubin thought, being he had good success buying John Henry from Snowden, he'd buy a couple more from him. He paid $35,000 for Gen Pillow, who wound up breaking his maiden in a cheap race at Belmont, then doing little after that. "Me like a jerk bought him and wound up getting rid of him for $5,000," Rubin said. The other horse, a filly, broke her maiden for $20,000 at the Meadowlands.

Although John Henry went winless in his next five starts, he did follow his allowance victory by finishing third, beaten two necks, in the Lamplighter Handicap at Monmouth; second to the top-class Darby Creek Road in the Hill Prince Handicap at Belmont; and second, beaten a head by that year's grass champion Mac Diarmida, in the Lexington Handicap at Belmont. John was now keeping company with some of the best turf horses in the country.

Saratoga was not as kind to John. Put back on the dirt and back in a sprint, he was outrun badly by Darby Creek Road, who sizzled seven furlongs in 1:20 2/5. Back on the turf ten days later, he finished fourth in a one and a sixteenth-mile allowance race. There was no

denying he had made an incredible turnaround since being put on the grass, but he still was a work in progress, with some rough edges to smooth before the final product emerged.

A return to Belmont Park certainly didn't hurt. On September 9, he won a seven-furlong allowance race on the grass by a length and a half in a sharp 1:22 flat. Then it was off to Arlington Park the following week for the Round Table Handicap. This looked like an excellent spot for John to win his first grass stakes. Donato, displeased with Angel Santiago's ride in the Lexington, had replaced him after the dirt race at Saratoga with Jose Amy.

It was no contest. Amy sent John right to front and set easy fractions over a course labeled good. John was sent off as the 1-2 favorite and ran like it. Just as he had in his first grass start, he pulverized his field and drew off to win by twelve lengths. Despite the victory, Rubin, incensed that Amy would vigorously whip John Henry while winning by twelve lengths, decided to replace him.

With Chicago conquered, it was off to California. John Henry ran twice at Santa Anita with a new rider,

Chuck Baltazar, aboard and didn't win either race. But he did turn in a huge effort to finish third in the Volante Handicap, beaten a half-length, despite getting into traffic problems. It was here, however, that the relationship between Donato and Rubin began to deteriorate. Over the years, both owner and trainer have declined to comment on the reasons. While Rubin has stuck to that, Donato claims it was about Rubin's refusal to pay worker's compensation in California, which had to come out of Donato's pocket.

Two weeks after returning from California, John was sent to Penn National, near Hershey, Pennsylvania, to run in the Chocolatetown Handicap, which was split into two divisions. With yet another new rider, Ray Broussard, John carried top weight of 124 pounds to victory as the 7-10 favorite. Although the margin was only one length, he was hand ridden through the stretch and never was in any real danger. Although the Chocolatetown hardly ranks with the stakes John would go on to win, Rubin considers this victory one of his most memorable.

Rubin was a chocolate fanatic, and when he was presented with the winning cup and saw that it was

filled with Hershey's Kisses, his mouth began to water. "The chairman of the board of Hershey's presented me with the cup," Rubin said, "and when I saw what was inside it, I was tongue-tied. I couldn't wait to take that damn silver off the chocolates and eat them. There were four of us at the table upstairs, and when we got back there, we ate the whole cup full of chocolates. After John Henry won his first Arlington Million, I was asked on national TV if it was the greatest thrill I've had in racing. I said it was one of them, along with winning the Chocolatetown Handicap. The chairman of Hershey's almost dropped dead when he heard it. After that, he'd send me a five-pound bar of chocolate every year. I was delirious."

It was now the beginning of November, and John had run nineteen times that year, thirteen of them for Donato and Rubin. This was hardly the same horse who began the year floundering at Fair Grounds and toiling through cheap claiming races. Donato felt John had had enough for one year and needed some time off.

"Sam wanted to run him in the Japan Racing Association Handicap at Laurel because he wanted to meet some people there," Donato said. "I didn't like the way he came out of the race at Penn National. He looked like he was a little off behind."

With their relationship now at its lowest, Rubin decided to change trainers and turned John Henry over to the veteran V. J. "Lefty" Nickerson. "To tell you the truth, I can't even remember why I made the change," Rubin said. "I just felt I wanted to make a change."

So, Bobby Donato joined the growing list of horsemen who found and then lost John Henry, unaware of their fleeting moment with greatness. Donato has all but faded from the pages of John Henry's life, and for that, he remains bitter. He stayed in New York until 1989 before trying his luck in California. But he was never able to get going there and gave up training from 1993 to 1995. In recent years, he suffered two heart attacks and an aneurysm. But still he returned to training, staying on the East Coast in the summer and Fair Grounds in the winter. He was content to keep three to five horses, but was unable to pick up any owners, and in the fall of 2000 he was down to one horse.

"When I was in New York in the eighties, people I knew called me the unknown man and the forgotten man," Donato said. "No one realized what I did with

John Henry. I put him on the grass. I stretched him out to two turns. I gave Lefty Nickerson a made stakes horse. Nobody handed me a made stakes horse. Jimmy Ferraro died a few years ago, and he was the one who really boosted me, because he knew what I did with that horse. Whenever someone would mention John Henry I never said anything. But Jimmy would say, 'Here's the guy who made John Henry.'

"Believe it or not, you might think I'm crazy, but I always rooted for the horse. I never had any malice toward him, because he had nothing to do with the owner. John Henry did nothing but good things for me, and he ran his heart out for me. What more could I ask?"

CHAPTER 6

Meet John Henry

John Henry entered the next phase of his life, a short haul away at Belmont Park where he was placed in Lefty Nickerson's barn. This would be the final stop before his journey to Ron McAnally and superstardom. Rubin said he chose Nickerson because of his directness and his sense of humor. "He didn't try to con me," Rubin said. The balding, veteran trainer believes it was because of his "handsomeness and curly hair."

Nickerson had won a number of major stakes in his career and had great success for Elmendorf Farm with horses like Big Spruce, who defeated Forego in the 1974 Marlboro Cup and Governor Stakes. "Somebody recommended Lefty to me, and I found him to be very straightforward," Rubin said.

"I met Sam one day in the clubhouse at Aqueduct," recalled Nickerson, who suffered a stroke several years ago and is now retired from training. "He asked me if I wanted to take the horse. He looked like a pretty ordinary horse, and he had a reputation of being pretty nasty. But I can't remember having any problems with him. I thought he was just a minor handicap horse."

John Henry's time with Nickerson did not turn out to be very memorable, as he accounted for only three allowance victories and a pair of seconds in stakes. He didn't make his first start of 1979 until May 26, finishing second in a six-furlong allowance race on the dirt. Nickerson ran him again at Monmouth, in a mile allowance on the dirt, and he won by fourteen lengths as the 4-5 favorite. After a horrendous performance in the Massachusetts Handicap, he was put back on the grass. Seconds in the Sunrise Handicap at Atlantic City and Sword Dancer Stakes at Belmont were followed by back-to-back allowance victories at Saratoga and Belmont. In between, John tried the dirt again, in the Capitol City Handicap at Penn National, but could only manage a fourth-place finish.

In his grass victory at Saratoga, John cruised to an impressive front-running score in a swift 1:46 2/5 for a mile and an eighth. "When he came back and beat a champion mare like Waya at Belmont I knew he was on his way," Nickerson said.

John was on his way all right, on his way to California and eventually the Hall of Fame.

In order to comprehend the amazing feats that are to follow and not simply dismiss them as something freakish, it is best to discover first just who John Henry is, and what enabled him to achieve greatness, and why he was so intent on destruction all his life. This actually was done when John was ten years old and attempting to make it back from suspensory problems.

In January of 1985, *Equus* magazine, a leading horse-training and -health publication, gathered a collection of veterinarians and scientists, a bloodstock expert, a psychic, an astrologer, and an equine awareness expert to perform studies on this equine enigma. Some spent time with John Henry at Santa Anita and others observed him on tape. Through their efforts, a picture began to take shape of an extraordinary athlete and personality.

Ron McAnally was skeptical at first. After all, who knew more about John Henry and what made him the champion he was? McAnally felt no scientific study could measure that indefinable quality known as heart.

But McAnally and readers of *Equus'* study soon would find out what it was about that heart, and other aspects of his outer and inner being, that separated John from other horses.

To try to understand John Henry's personality and explore the source of the hostility that had gnawed away at him since he was a baby, *Equus* brought in psychic Nancy Regalmuto, who used her prognosticating powers in the field of handicapping horses. Regalmuto spent two hours with John, and at one point the two just stared at each other, "conversing." John stood there motionless as if he were in a trance, with his eyes half-closed.

"I thought she was some kind of a nut when she said she wanted to interview the horse," McAnally said. "For forty-five minutes she looked right at him and asked him questions, all the while patting him. The horse never moved the whole time. She said she could tell what he was feeling just by touching him and talking to him."

In the first session, in which Regalmuto picked up sensory signals with her hands, she told of a spoiled, stubborn individual, but one with extreme intelligence, who wanted to have things his own way. She also said the tenacity he displayed in his encounters with humans was the same trait he used so effectively on the racetrack, accounting for his incredible will to win. She also picked up that John's strength and sound constitution came from his dam Once Double. But John also conveyed to her a concern he had about an attack of colic his dam had recently suffered. A subsequent check with the farm where she resided confirmed that Once Double had indeed come down with an intestinal condition several weeks earlier.

Other conclusions from Regalmuto's conversations with John were that he felt he was a better racehorse at this time in his life because he had spent his early years fighting the thought of being a racehorse. He also felt people got in his way and wanted to control the things he did, and he had no tolerance for them. But there was one bizarre story John supposedly told that was relayed by Regalmuto in such detail, it certainly provided ammunition for the skeptics.

Speaking in John's own words, the story told of a best friend John had at "one of the first farms" where he resided. This horse couldn't run very well, but always tried, and he would often lecture John about the realities of racing, telling him not to fight so hard and accept the fact that his life was not his own. John wouldn't believe him, feeling he eventually would win. John told Regalmuto, "One day they came in and put him to sleep in front of all of us. It was sad. He tried so hard to do the right thing for humans, and humans didn't care. I realized how heartless and cold humans could be. I guess I rebelled after his death."

But John said the more he thought about it, the more he realized that his friend was right. He accepted the ways of the world and came to realize, "We have no real choices but only one path to follow — pleasing humans. The only real win we have is our own survival."

Regalmuto's interpretations and John's strange tale were printed in *Equus*. One of the skeptics was McAnally. "I disregarded what she said. I really paid no attention to it," he said. But McAnally did give credence to some of the scientific studies. "They helped to confirm some of the things we suspected about John Henry, but really had no way of proving," he said.

Measurements of John Henry's frame and legs taken by Dr. Matthew Mackay-Smith, veterinary surgeon and *Equus'* medical editor, showed that the horse's legs were about an inch longer than one would expect from a horse his height, which could partially account for John's long, fluid strides. They also revealed a horse of near-perfect proportions. John Henry's measurements were computer analyzed by Ken Trimble of the Computer Horse Breeders Association. Judging from the twenty-one measurements taken, Trimble got a clear picture of how John Henry was put together. Going by the balance among power, body weight, and stride, he concluded that of the thousands of horses he had analyzed, John Henry was right there at the top, scoring only one point lower than the highest rating he had ever given. He noted that the power in John's hindquarters combined with his superior shoulder development and muscle texture made the horse as close to a perfect racehorse as possible.

Veterinarian Norman Rantanen of Echo Affiliates Inc., who had used a specially designed ultrasound imager to determine the heart size of over a thousand racehorses, couldn't even fit John Henry's entire left ventricle onto the imager. Rantanen was able to measure the left ventricle at approximately twenty centimeters, which placed the horse in the upper three percent of the stakes-winning horses he had evaluated. He said

that John's heart was twenty percent to twenty-five per-cent larger than the average equine heart, which enabled him to pump more blood through his system, increasing his aerobic power. This allowed him to carry his speed over long distances with minimum accumulation of lactic acid and other by-products of fatigue.

John also was believed to have a large spleen, because of an extremely low resting red blood cell count. As stated in the *Equus* report, "only a good-sized spleen could hold enough red cells in reserve to fuel John Henry's needs in the heat of competition."

Dr. George Pratt, professor of electrical engineering and computer science at Massachusetts Institute of Technology, who had been studying the locomotion of the racehorse for eight years, observed John Henry's stride. After watching and analyzing four of John's races, Pratt concluded: "His gait is a thing of ice-cold efficiency. Not a single wasted motion. As soon as his feet come off the ground, they are going forward. He seems to pump away with the head, enhancing his one-breath-per-stride air exchange. John Henry just does not fall apart and show ordinary signs of fatigue. No climbing at the finish, no bearing out or in. The changes of lead are wonderfully smooth — a Ferrari going through the gears. He often changes leads when he's near the finish line. It provides a tiny advantage, a nose or less. The way he times it, it looks as if he knows what he's doing. His ears go up just as soon as he has a race in the bag."

Other studies, such as bone density, also showed John to be well above normal. Linda Tellington-Jones, founder of T.E.A.M. (Tellington-Jones Equine Awareness Movements), used her sense of touch and knowledge of equine anatomy to conclude that John had a strong self-image and was "constantly reaffirming his superiority and determination to call the shots. It's almost as though he's just checking to make sure everyone realizes who's in command."

In summarizing all the studies, Mackay-Smith said, "Of all the factors involved in John Henry's success, his personality is perhaps the most obvious. All of the members of our panel of experts were instantly aware of his powerful presence, whether they were stallside or watching him on film." Mackay-Smith put all the findings together and came up with a picture of a horse that is "self-confident, aloof, alert, studious, wise and, it

must be said, more than a bit theatrical. At the risk of anthropomorphisizing, he's one horse who will never fall victim to an equine identity crisis. That look in his eyes tells you John Henry knows exactly who he is."

That was the John Henry who was about to explode through the pages of history. But with all the scientific findings, it took someone close to the horse to convert all the data into a single simple sentence. Dr. Jack Robbins, who would be John Henry's veterinarian for the five years he spent with McAnally, put it best when he said at the end of the horse's career, "Ol' John threw the book away a long time ago."

CHAPTER 7

How The West Was Won

It was September of 1979, and in New York that meant a time for the crowning of champions. Two of the sport's all-time greats, Affirmed and Spectacular Bid, were on a collision course to decide Horse of the Year honors in the Jockey Club Gold Cup. In the turf division, Greentree Stable's Bowl Game was about to lock up the championship with victories in the Man o' War Stakes and Turf Classic.

For the owners and trainers of allowance and small-time stakes horses such as John Henry, it was either throwing them to the wolves at distances and weights beyond their best or skipping town. Winter would soon be approaching, anyway, which meant an end to turf racing. And Aqueduct's inner dirt track was not the place for riches and glory.

Rubin had a decision to make. He had rented a place

in Florida for the winter, and asked Nickerson about sending John Henry down there where he could see him run, promising him that he would get the horse back in the spring. Nickerson, who had decided to remain in New York for the winter, felt that California would be better for John Henry, especially since he had run well at Santa Anita in the past.

While mulling the situation, Rubin happened to be talking to a friend of his, a man he knew simply as Johnson, who ran the binocular rental stand at the New York tracks. When Rubin told him he was looking to ship John Henry to a warm climate for the winter, Johnson said, "Why don't you send him to California? That's where the real grass racing is."

California was now firmly implanted in Rubin's brain, and he began looking West. One day, he was sitting in his box at Belmont Park when a friend pointed out Charlie Whittingham sitting nearby. This was too good to be true. Who better to train John Henry than the legendary "Bald Eagle"? Rubin decided to seize the opportunity. He went over to Whittingham and introduced himself.

"Mr. Whittingham, my name is Sam Rubin," he said.

"I have a horse I want to send to California, and I was wondering if you'd be interested in training him? His name is John Henry."

Whittingham barely blinked an eye. He nonchalantly replied, "Yeah, I know the horse. I'll think about it and get back to you."

Rubin never heard from him. "That was the most polite brush-off I ever got," Rubin said.

Whittingham's brush-off would come back to haunt the trainer. Over the next five years, a total of nineteen Whittingham-trained horses would fall victim to the horse he so nonchalantly dismissed that day at Belmont. Whittingham soon began to accept the situation with his usual philosophical and humorous approach. In the 1984 Sunset Handicap, a frustrated Whittingham saddled four horses against John Henry, all of them top-class, including 1982 Kentucky Derby winner Gato Del Sol. Before the race, he was quoted as saying, "I may not beat him, but at least I've got him surrounded."

But once again, Whittingham couldn't beat him. In commenting that year on John Henry's longevity, Whittingham said, "Not only is he beating my best horses, he's beating their children. Goddammit, he beat

Balzac when I had him, and I've got two-year-olds in the barn sired by Balzac, and John Henry is still running."

Whittingham's most famous line came before a race against John Henry, when someone asked him whether he thought he had a chance to beat the old horse. "Beat him?" the then seventy-two-year-old Whittingham said. "Hell, I'm just trying to outlive him."

When Rubin told Nickerson he would send the horse to California, Nickerson recommended his old friend Ron McAnally. The forty-seven-year-old McAnally was one of the most respected trainers in California, but had yet to reach the national spotlight. His biggest victories came in 1976 when he saddled An Act to win the Santa Anita Derby and Pay Tribute to win the Hollywood Gold Cup. He had made his presence felt in New York well before that, winning the Champagne Stakes at Belmont with Donut King in 1961, knocking off the East's top two-year-olds Jaipur, Sir Gaylord, and Crimson Satan.

Born in 1932 in Covington, Kentucky, McAnally was five when his mother died, and with his father unable to care for their five children, Ron and his two brothers and two sisters were sent to an orphanage to be raised. Reggie Cornell, his uncle by marriage, gave McAnally his start in racing, letting the teenager walk hots at Rockingham Park in New Hampshire. Cornell, who would become a top trainer and saddle the charismatic and enigmatic Silky Sullivan to win the 1957 Santa Anita Derby before going to work for Calumet Farm, kept moving McAnally around, so he could learn from the bottom. While working at Santa Anita, McAnally remembered looking into the neighboring barn and seeing another young groom mucking out stalls. He was so small, McAnally wondered why he wasn't a jockey. Some thirty years later, those two grooms, McAnally and Bill Shoemaker, would team up to win America's first million-dollar horse race.

A short time later, McAnally received his draft notice, and instead of being drafted, he enlisted in the Air Force. He hated every minute of it, almost dying from pneumonia while stationed in Alaska. When McAnally eventually got married and his wife became pregnant, he received his discharge.

"I had a responsibility now, and with racing involving so much traveling, I had to find something else to do with my life," McAnally said. "I attended the Ohio

Mechanics Institute studying electrical engineering, and hated that as much as the Air Force. While attending classes I drove a Coca-Cola delivery truck to make a living. I always had racing stored in the back of my mind. I wanted to go back so badly I could taste it."

McAnally and his first wife had different lifestyles, and eventually they divorced, with McAnally immediately heading back to the track.

While grooming horses for owner-trainer Sidney Sylvestor Shupper at the old Tropical Park in Florida, McAnally became friends with fellow groom Lefty Nickerson.

McAnally eventually went to California, where he took out his trainer's license. He saddled his first winner, Hemet Star, at Hollywood Park in 1958, and won his first stakes, the San Fernando, with King O' Turf in 1960.

In the fall of 1979, McAnally had not won a race of national significance since his two big scores in '76. But he still was having great success training stakes winners such as Queen to Be, Replant, and Syncopate for Max Gluck's Elmendorf Farm, which was sending him about twenty two-year-olds every year. Ironically, it was Nickerson who trained Elmendorf's New York division, and he too had enjoyed good success for that farm with stakes horses such as Big Spruce.

The two friends had kept in touch with each other since their days grooming horses. One day, Nickerson called McAnally and told him he had a nice horse he wanted to send him and that he should expect a call from the horse's owner.

The following morning, McAnally was in his tack room at Santa Anita when Rubin called and introduced himself. He told McAnally that he'd like to send him John Henry, and that he had nominated the gelding to the Carleton F. Burke Handicap at a mile and a quarter on the turf on October 14, which was only several days away. The arrangement was that McAnally would train John Henry in California, and whenever the horse returned to New York to race, Nickerson would saddle him.

All McAnally knew about John Henry was what Nickerson had told him: "He's a nice horse, probably up to a mile and an eighth, but certainly not a world beater." McAnally entered him in the Burke, but with the air cargo workers on strike, there was a problem getting a flight to Los Angeles. Just when it looked like John Henry would miss the race, a flight was found at the last

minute, and the gelding was off to California. He arrived at Barn 99 at four in the morning the day of the race. McAnally arrived a short time later and went around the corner of the barn to the first stall to look in on his new arrival. He couldn't believe the horse was going to have to run a mile and a quarter that same afternoon.

Nor was he enamored with the little gelding as a physical specimen. "I never would have bought him as a yearling," McAnally said. "He was a very ordinary-looking horse and very weak boned under the knee. He didn't have the kind of bone any horseman would like to see."

As surprised as McAnally was about the turn of events, he was even more surprised when John Henry battled head and head on the lead most of the way under jockey Darrel McHargue and held on tenaciously to finish second. This was a big improvement from the previous year, when John had finished sixth in the same race for Bobby Donato. By getting beat only a length and quarter in 1:59 1/5, over a distance at which he had never won, John had McAnally thinking that maybe this was a better horse than he was led to believe. "All I kept thinking was, 'My goodness, what kind of horse do we have here?' " McAnally said.

By now John was no longer the wild, destructive beast he had been in his youth. But he still was not a horse to mess with. "They told me he was nasty, which he was," McAnally said. "He was the kind of horse you didn't want to fool around with. Some horses you can play with and tease, and they'll pin their ears and snap at you, but they really didn't mean it. With him, he meant it."

McAnally thought back to another ornery horse he had several years earlier: an Argentine import named Cruiser II. A gelding like John, Cruiser II was a horse who struck fear into those around him. McAnally felt the best way to get along with a horse like that was to smother him with kindness. He gave him sugar, carrots, and other treats in an effort to win his friendship. "The better we treated him, the better he'd run," McAnally said. Cruiser II kept improving and wound up winning the Sunset Handicap and Del Mar Invitational Handicap.

McAnally tried the same approach with John, and like Cruiser II, he responded. "I just wanted him to know that we were on his side," McAnally said. "I figured if we gave him a lot of tender, loving care, he, in turn, would convert that nastiness he had when he

was young into competitiveness on the racetrack."

What also helped was having three superior horsemen around the horse every day — groom Jose Mercado, exercise rider Lewis Cenicola, and assistant trainer Eduardo Inda. Cenicola, however, would not get on John until the fall of 1980.

Mercado, a native of Mexico, began working for McAnally in the early seventies. When he was given John Henry to groom, it didn't take him long to realize he was going be tested every day. One of John's favorite ploys while being rubbed down was to inch his way slowly across the stall. He'd keep moving Mercado back until the groom found himself trapped against the wall, with no way out. Mercado, who was one of McAnally's stronger grooms, knew very well that it wasn't healthy to be at the mercy of John Henry, so he had to use his strength and a few choice words to get him to back off. But over the years, the two grew to respect each other, and there was no one who was closer to John or knew him better than Mercado.

"In the beginning, he was very mean, and I had to be a little rough with him at times," Mercado said. "It was the only way to gain his respect. Once I did, we got along very well. I gave him lots of sugar and carrots. He did give me a little kick one time after I first got him, but in all the time we were together, he never once bit me. I really miss him a lot, especially when they run the big stakes races."

After the Burke, McAnally ran John back three weeks later in a division of the Henry P. Russell Handicap, and the four-year-old had little trouble wiring his field by three and a quarter lengths as the 7-10 favorite. His final start of the year came in the Bay Meadows Handicap, and after making a huge run from eighth to take the lead at the eighth pole, he was caught in the final seventy yards by the six-year-old New Zealand-bred gelding Leonotis, who was saddled by an up-and-coming young trainer from the Quarter Horse game named D. Wayne Lukas.

After an eleven-race campaign in 1979, John was ready to jump right into the 1980 season. Now five, John still had not made his mark in major races, having only four minor stakes victories to his credit. That was about to change.

Over the next five months, John Henry, out of nowhere, went on a tear that saw him win six consecutive major events, culminating with two of the most prestigious turf races in the country, the marathon San Juan

Capistrano and the Hollywood Invitational Turf Handicap. This turn of events awakened a part of John's past that had all but faded into a distant memory. The blurred images from another lifetime suddenly came alive. From Verna and Fred Lehmann, John and Jean Callaway, Bubba Snowden, Akiko McVarish, Phil Marino, Colleen Madere, Dorthea Lingo, Bobby Donato, and enough veterinarians to staff the New Bolton Medical Center came a collective gasp that could be heard in New York and Kentucky and down to Louisiana.

John Henry began his streak in the one and an eighth-mile San Gabriel Handicap on New Year's Day when he out battled Smasher to win by a head. John carried 123 pounds and was giving Smasher twelve pounds. McAnally knew John Henry could run on dirt. Hoping that little fact had escaped Santa Anita racing secretary Lou Eilken's notice, he entered him in the one and a quarter-mile San Marcos Handicap. "We were just trying to get some weight off him," McAnally said. But instead of taking weight off or keeping John Henry at the same weight, Eilken raised him a pound. Only four showed up to face John, and they never had a chance. John went right to the front and coasted to an easy two and a half-length score in 2:01 3/5, conceding eleven pounds to runner-up El Fantastico.

The next logical spot was the one and a half-mile San Luis Obispo Handicap. The Santa Anita condition book normally listed the closing dates for nominations to upcoming stakes. But on the day the San Luis Obispo closed, there were three other stakes closing and the condition book didn't have room for it. The important date was only printed on the overnights. Both McAnally and McHargue's agent, Scotty McLellan, missed the deadline and didn't realize the oversight until it was too late. The San Luis Rey was not for another two months, and McAnally needed to find a race for John Henry before then. He and McLellan went through condition books from several other tracks and noticed that the Hialeah Turf Cup had supplementary nominations that weren't due until February 16.

Rubin put up the $5,000 supplementary fee, and John headed back East to Hialeah. The move didn't seem like a wise one when John drew post ten in the ten-horse field. Sitting in the boxes was another short-lived character in the John Henry saga, Joe Taub, who had told Rubin that day at Aqueduct that he had no interest in cheap horses before setting him up with Jimmy Ferraro. Taub told McAnally the whole story of how he got Rubin and Ferraro together, then sat back and rooted for his friend's horse. Sent off as the 2-1 second choice behind Producer, John Henry, as McAnally had feared, got hung very wide on the turn. He was kept under pressure the entire race while stalking the pace, and despite going wide through-out the one and a half-mile race, held off Dancing Master to win by a half-length.

Back at Santa Anita, a huge crowd of 56,614 showed up on March 16 to see John Henry draw off to a length and a half victory over Relaunch in the San Luis Rey, equaling Fiddle Isle's course record of 2:23 for a mile and a half. Finishing at the rear of the pack were two horses — Flying Paster and Golden Act — still sporting the scars from past battles with Spectacular Bid.

It was obvious that a new turf star was emerging on the scene, and it was time to take another leap forward in the $200,000 San Juan Capistrano over the grueling distance of about a mile and three-quarters. McAnally gave John nothing but long, slow works to build his stamina and didn't even blow him out before the race. Sent off as a lukewarm 2-1 favorite and carrying top weight of 126 pounds, John pulled McHargue to the lead and never completely relaxed. Every time a horse came up to him, John would grab the bit a little tighter and take off again. Four horses took a run at him, but he was tenacious and held his lead to the wire, defeating Fiestero, in receipt of twelve pounds, by a length and a quarter. The horse who just months earlier was considered by his trainer as a nice little horse up to a mile and an eighth, was now the leading turf horse in the country and a winner at a mile and three-quarters.

After winning a tough battle with Balzac in the $250,000 Hollywood Invitational, under 128 pounds, it was decided to send John Henry back East.

"Sam had been doing a lot of traveling out to California, and there wasn't much more for John on the turf out here," McAnally said. Both McAnally and Nickerson were splitting the ten-percent winner's share, as McAnally thought it was the only fair thing to do. After all, he wouldn't have had the horse if it weren't for Nickerson. It was an arrangement that McAnally would keep all through John Henry's career.

So John returned to Nickerson at Belmont, only to finish second in the Bowling Green Handicap and

John Henry was an unwanted vagabond who became a beloved hero. He amazed racing experts and delighted fans with his courage, durability, and longevity. At the age of nine, John Henry earned his second Horse of the Year title and closed out a career that numbered thirty-nine wins in eighty-three starts and an amazing $6.6 million in earnings.

Although John Henry's pedigree is considered weak, there is plenty of quality to be found. His sire, Ole Bob Bowers, equaled the world record for nine furlongs in the Tanforan Handicap (top). Prince Blessed (above right), sire of Ole Bob Bowers, won the Hollywood Gold Cup. John Henry's broodmare sire, Double Jay (right), was a champion two-year-old and later a four-time leading broodmare sire.

John Henry himself wasn't much to look at as a baby (below), leading to his sale as a yearling.

Robert Lehmann (above with wife, Verna) liked to build things, including his Golden Chance Farm (below) and a bell tower and mausoleum in front of his home (right). The Lehmanns and son Fred (above right) were no strangers to racing success, having won the 1970 Kentucky Derby with Dust Commander, but they had no way of knowing that a scrawny son of Once Double would become their farm's biggest star.

John Callaway (above with John Henry) and his wife Jean paid $1,100 for the then-yearling. They sold John Henry the next year for $2,200 to Harold "Bubba" Snowden Jr. (left), who ended up owning him three separate times. In between, John Henry was owned by Louisiana native Colleen Madere and trained by Phil Marino, who sent John Henry out for his first victory, a maiden race at Jefferson Downs (top, Marino on far right, Madere holding the winner).

John Henry partnered with numerous jockeys during his career, including Darrel McHargue (above right) and Laffit Pincay Jr. (above left), who rode John as his star was rising, and Bill Shoemaker (top) and Chris McCarron (right), who teamed with the gelding for his greatest victories.

After his time with Phil Marino, John Henry went through the barns of several other trainers on his way to the top. First was Bobby Donato (above left), then came V. J. "Lefty" Nickerson (above right), who alternated training the horse with longtime friend Ron McAnally. At the end of 1980, John Henry stayed in McAnally's care for good and together the two (left) made history.

A bicycle salesman from New York, Sam Rubin admittedly knew nothing about horses when he purchased John Henry for $25,000 in 1978. John would go on to earn eight Eclipse Awards for Rubin and his wife, Dorothy (right), including the leading owner Eclipse in 1981.

Several members of Ron McAnally's team connected with John Henry, including assistant trainer Eduardo Inda (above right) and exercise rider Lewis Cenicola (left). But none was closer than groom Jose Mercado (above left, in the 1986 Eclipse Award-winning photograph).

John Henry's victory in the Chocolatetown
Handicap (below) thrilled the chocolate-
loving Sam Rubin. John won the
Chocolatetown and the Round Table
Handicap (right) for trainer Bobby Donato.
The gelding's first stakes win for Ron
McAnally came in a division of the 1979
Henry P. Russell Handicap at Santa Anita
(above).

In 1980 at the age of five, John Henry finally hit his true stride and put together a six-race string of graded victories, including the San Marcos on the dirt (left), the Hialeah Turf Cup (below), and the San Juan Capistrano (bottom). He closed out his season with the first of three consecutive wins in the Oak Tree Invitational (opposite).

In 1981, John Henry continued his ascent to the top of the racing world with triumphs in the San Luis Obispo (above), the prestigious Santa Anita Handicap (right), and the Hollywood Invitational (top).

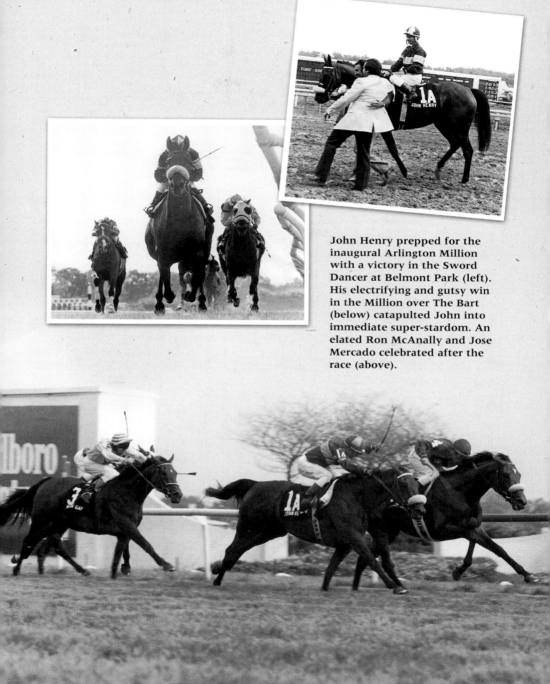

John Henry prepped for the inaugural Arlington Million with a victory in the Sword Dancer at Belmont Park (left). His electrifying and gutsy win in the Million over The Bart (below) catapulted John into immediate super-stardom. An elated Ron McAnally and Jose Mercado celebrated after the race (above).

John Henry seemed to know when he was being photographed or admired by his adoring public (above, in the 1983 Eclipse Award-winning photo). Fans continued to see the familiar shadow roll bob along in the stretch as John added more victories, including, from top to bottom, the 1981 Jockey Club Gold Cup, 1982 Santa Anita Handicap, and 1983 American Handicap.

At the ripe old age of nine, John Henry had perhaps his best season, winning six stakes, including his second Arlington Million (above) and the Turf Classic at Belmont (right). He closed out his incredible career at the Meadowlands with a win in the Ballantine's Scotch Classic (below).

John Henry received a hero's welcome and a greeting from Governor Martha Layne Collins (above) when he was retired to the Kentucky Horse Park in 1985. Wes Lanter (top right) managed the Horse Park's Hall of Champions at the time.
John still receives visits from old friends, such as Ron McAnally (right), and fans who will never forget how John Henry overcame the odds to become one of racing's greatest champions. John Henry's first Million victory is immortalized in the sculpture "Against All Odds."

Sword Dancer Stakes. But he turned in courageous performances in defeat, battling hard on the lead all the way. While John was cooling out in the test barn after being beaten by Tiller in the Sword Dancer, Tiller's trainer David Whiteley looked at this little package of dynamite and remarked, "What a game horse he is, what a grand competitor."

When McHargue suffered an injury after the Sword Dancer, Angel Cordero Jr. replaced him. In John's first start under Cordero, the gelding gamely won the one and a quarter-mile Brighton Beach Handicap by a neck in 1:59 2/5. It was then decided to take another crack at the dirt in the Jockey Club Gold Cup, and although John ran a strong race, he couldn't handle that year's three-year-old champion, Temperence Hill, who beat him by five and a half lengths. That was the end of Cordero's short stint as John Henry's rider, as Laffit Pincay replaced him. The Turf Classic looked like a good spot for John, but the course came up a bog after heavy rains. Unable to use his graceful strides and get into a good rhythm on soft going, John Henry struggled home a well-beaten third. It was time to return to McAnally, this time for good.

JOHN HENRY

CHAPTER 8

The Road To Stardom

John Henry's autumn excursion to New York had resulted in only one victory in five starts. Now back in the friendly confines of Barn 99 at Santa Anita, John was introduced to a new acquaintance, who would become as familiar a sight on the gelding as Dotsam Stable's brown and blue colors. For the next four years, John's back would become a second home to Lewis Cenicola.

Cenicola began exercising horses for McAnally in 1971, and before that had worked for Buster Millerick, Jay Robbins, and William J. "Buddy" Hirsch, for whom he exercised Hall of Fame filly Gallant Bloom. By 1979, he had been around the daily grind of racetrack life for fourteen years and felt as if he were getting burned out. He decided to take some time off to try to rekindle the enthusiasm he once had for the sport. In the winter of 1980, after being away for about a year, he returned to

McAnally. That fall, John Henry's regular exercise rider, Tony Rubalcada, had to return home to Mexico, and Cenicola was given the seat on what was about to become racing's most exalted throne.

Cenicola's morning jaunts aboard John Henry were more like leisurely strolls on a lazy summer day. John was in no hurry to get his daily chores done, only to return to the confinement of the dreaded stall. It often would take him forty-five minutes to get from his barn to the track. He'd make numerous stops along the way just to look around and soak up the atmosphere, as he had done years earlier, grazing along the road at Jefferson Downs. McAnally's philosophy was simple: Whatever John wanted to do was fine with him. That way, everyone stayed happy and healthy.

Cenicola insists that John remembered every track he visited, and even which stall he was in. "Every time he returned to a track, he'd stop at the exact same places," Cenicola said. "If he was put in a different stall, he'd always slow up when he got to the previous stall he was in and just walk around there for a while before going to the track. He was just an amazing horse and extremely intelligent. He knew how to take care of himself."

After returning to McAnally, John ran in the Oak Tree Invitational Stakes on November 16. After uncharacteristically dropping far off the pace, he seemed hopelessly out of it. As McAnally watched this debacle unfold, the same thoughts kept nagging at him: "What did I do? I shouldn't have run him. I went to the well once too often." Just then, John exploded and charged relentlessly down the stretch, making up an amazing seven lengths in the final furlong, to blow by Balzac and win going away by a length and a half in a swift 2:23 2/5.

John Henry had concluded his five-year-old campaign with eight victories in twelve starts for earnings of $925,217, earning him his first Eclipse Award as champion male grass horse. Rubin decided to keep John Henry with McAnally for good.

From age four to five, John Henry had undergone a dramatic transformation from useful allowance and small-stakes horse to champion. He was now about to undergo yet another major transformation, from champion to super horse.

John spent the rest of November and December taking it easy and basically just recharging his batteries. A

sharp mile work in the latter part of January got his mind back on running, and subsequent works at a mile and an eighth and a mile and a quarter had him primed for his first start of the year, the mile and a half San Luis Obispo on February 16. Racing secretary Lou Eilken didn't make things easy for John, assigning him 127 pounds, which was quite a load for the first start of the year. It was no contest, as Laffit Pincay put John on the lead and he ran his five opponents into the ground, winning by a length and a half.

McAnally's strategy over the winter was to point for the granddaddy of them all, the Santa Anita Handicap, hoping once again to get some weight off by running on the dirt. Among those he was up against was Flying Paster, who was riding a three-race winning streak after spending most of 1980 staring at the big gray rump of Spectacular Bid. Another tough opponent was the defending champion older mare Glorious Song, who had been the only horse in 1980 to make The Bid raise a sweat, finishing a length and three-quarters behind the great horse in the Amory Haskell Handicap at Monmouth Park.

Despite having to face a field of top-class horses on

their surface, John still picked up a pound to 128, receiving one pound from Flying Paster. Glorious Song was dropping eleven pounds from her neck defeat under 130 in the Santa Margarita Handicap. The anticipated battle among the best grass horse, best dirt horse, and best mare brought out a huge crowd of 66,560. Breaking from post three, John ran into traffic problems early and got shuffled back to sixth. When Pincay saw an opening at the three-sixteenths pole, he gunned John Henry through. Flying Paster was in retreat, and Glorious Song wasn't doing enough to threaten. John roared by his stablemate King Go Go, then drew clear to win by a length in a sharp 1:59 2/5 for the mile and a quarter.

Visions of Horse of the Year now swirled through McAnally's head. The San Luis Rey on March 29 was next, and because of the weight-for-age conditions, John was able to shed two pounds from his Big Cap win. He was an overwhelming 1-5 favorite and won easily by two and a quarter lengths over Obraztsovy.

Sam Rubin, meanwhile, was having a ball, raking in the riches and basking in the glory from his $25,000 purchase, which he called the "steal of the century."

Once a week he'd call McAnally just to see how things were going. "Ron was so trustworthy and so caring," Rubin said. "He is truly a lover of animals. We fell in love with him and his family. After we gave him John Henry, we realized we had something special. Every time the horse would win, we'd just say, 'My God!' We were in shock over what had had happened to us."

But the shock was just beginning. McAnally passed on the San Juan Capistrano when heavy rains turned the strip of dirt track the horses had to run over into a sloppy mess. By missing the Capistrano, McAnally had to run John Henry in the Hollywood Invitational off a seven-week layoff. He was forced to train him harder than usual, but John thrived on work, just as he thrived on racing. The training paid off, as John, carrying 130 pounds, outfought the hard-knocking Caterman by three-quarters of a length.

John Henry could do nothing wrong, and McAnally and Rubin decided to buck the odds by putting him back on the dirt and going for the $500,000 pot of gold in the Hollywood Gold Cup. John would have to carry 130 pounds again and run over a deeper, sandier surface than he was used to at Santa Anita.

Before the race John was given a new set of shoes, but the blacksmith took a little too much of the frog off. Although horses have no feeling in the frog, which supports the bottom of the foot, it still may have been enough to make John a little uncomfortable during the running of the race. All this conspired against the horse, and it didn't take long after the start of the race for Pincay to sense that John wasn't moving well over the track. Racing in mid-pack and in tight quarters, he managed to close ground, but had to settle for fourth, beaten less than three lengths. With five straight wins behind him, John had gotten used to a quick stopover in the winner's circle for a little picture posing before heading back to the barn. But this time, when Pincay dismounted on the track and Mercado attempted to take him back to the barn, John figured he'd better set him straight, and headed directly for the winner's circle. When McAnally and Mercado pulled him away and tried to steer him in the right direction, a disgruntled John Henry made his displeasure known, lashing back a few times with his hind legs. Sure, go ahead and tell John he lost.

John had become a real ham and loved having his

picture taken. Whenever he'd see a camera aimed at him or heard a shutter click, he'd snap his head in that direction. He knew when people were looking at him. In 1983, the Eclipse Award-winning photograph showed John staring at his adoring public.

With the beginning of summer, McAnally looked ahead to the biggest prize of all, the inaugural running of the Arlington Million, America's first million-dollar horserace. But that was still two and a half months away, and a trip back East for the Sword Dancer Stakes at Belmont was first on the agenda. Frank E. "Jimmy" Kilroe, Santa Anita's vice president of racing, had convinced McAnally to tackle a weight-for-age race in New York to help John Henry's cause for Horse of the Year. Ten days before the race, however, Pincay was suspended for careless riding, causing him to miss the Sword Dancer. McAnally found out Bill Shoemaker was available and quickly signed on the Hall of Fame rider.

The first time Shoemaker worked John Henry, McAnally was interested in his opinion of the horse. As Shoemaker dismounted, McAnally asked him, "So, what did you think of him?" The Shoe simply replied, "He's a pro."

McAnally then bid a temporary farewell to John, putting him on a plane for New York and the barn of his old trainer Lefty Nickerson, who still was responsible for the horse whenever he journeyed to the Big Apple. McAnally, who was now a self-admitted worrywart when it came to John, decided to spend his forty-ninth birthday in New York to see his horse run. John toyed with his four outclassed rivals to win by three and a half lengths.

Following the Sword Dancer, John rejoined McAnally's troops at Del Mar racetrack near San Diego to prepare for the Arlington Million. The Rubins came out to the track one afternoon while on vacation. When Sam saw Pincay, he went over to say hello, but Pincay walked right by him without saying a word. "You have to understand Laffit," McAnally said. "He was dieting heavily at that time and his mind was focused strictly on riding. When he was like that, he'd very seldom speak to anybody. After being ignored by Laffit, Sam felt as if he had been embarrassed and told me he wanted to switch riders."

Shortly after, it was announced that Shoemaker would replace Pincay on John Henry. But ten days

before the Arlington Million, the McAnally team faced a major crisis. John had gone out for a gallop that morning, and McAnally noticed he wasn't moving quite right. John appeared to be fine back at the barn, but at around 10:15, shortly after McAnally left for the morning, Eduardo Inda discovered the horse was noticeably off in his left foreleg. He immediately contacted Dr. Jack Robbins, who came over to check John out.

"He was very, very sensitive at the juncture of the cannon bone and the ankle, on the outside of the leg," Robbins said. "You couldn't put any pressure on it."

McAnally was summoned to the barn, and it was decided to run a set of X-rays. Del Mar had its own clinic, and it was much more thorough having the X-rays taken there as opposed to using a portable machine. All horses brought in for X-rays were recorded, so McAnally and Robbins had to do some fast thinking. The sight of John Henry having X-rays taken ten days before the Arlington Million was sure to create quite a stir, so they decided to bring him over and register him under another name. "We wanted to avoid a panic," McAnally said.

"We obviously didn't want anyone to know about it,"

Robbins added. "It's possible we could have been dealing with the beginning of a fractured cannon bone."

The X-rays, however, revealed no fracture. Robbins palpated the area and felt it might be some slight ligament damage. He told McAnally, "Let's take a shot and inject his ligament with some cortisone." McAnally agreed, and John was injected with Depo-medrol. The next morning, he was walking perfectly and the sensitivity was gone. McAnally took it slow with John over the next two days, just galloping him to see how the leg progressed. There was no sign he had even had an injury. But, with the Million now only a week away, it was imperative he have a strong work, which would serve two purposes: to get him sharp for the big race and see how the leg stood up under pressure.

"Doc, we've got a very important work coming up," McAnally told Robbins. "If we don't work him, he's not going to run in the Arlington Million."

The Saturday before the Million, John worked on the main track with Shoemaker aboard. "I was scared to death," Robbins said. "Even though the X-rays were negative, you never know if it's a fracture coming on or not." John went out there and had jaws dropping,

as he blazed a mile and an eighth in 1:46 3/5. A stunned McAnally told Robbins, "If he wins the Million, I'm going to thank you on national TV" — a promise he would keep.

JOHN HENRY

CHAPTER 9

One In A Million

All systems were go. A few days after being given a clean bill of health, John departed for Chicago, accompanied by Mercado and Inda and stablemate Super Moment. Cenicola had left earlier to prepare for the horse's arrival. NBC had been contracted to televise the one and a quarter mile race over the lush Arlington turf course, and the event was getting tremendous coverage both nationally and internationally. The race was the brainchild of then-Arlington owner David A. "Sonny" Werblin, who felt America needed a rich turf event in the summer. There was little for mile and a quarter turf horses in America and Europe, and Arlington would provide a neutral spot that would not favor California or New York horses.

Among those coming from Europe were Argument, runner-up in the 1980 Prix de l'Arc de Triomphe, and the

1980 and 1981 French Oaks winners Mrs. Penny and Madam Gay. The latter also had finished second in the '81 English Oaks. The leading American contenders in addition to John Henry and Super Moment were United Nations Handicap winner Key to Content; the local favorite Rossi Gold, winner of three stakes at the Arlington meeting; and Charlie Whittingham's classy mare Kilijaro.

McAnally knew John would be the big favorite, and all he wanted was a firm turf course and a good post position, so there'd be no excuses. On the day entries were drawn, he and Debbie, who still were in California, had just finished packing their bags and were about to leave when they received a phone call from a good friend, Bill Kolberg, a publicist for Santa Anita and Del Mar.

"Ron, I'm calling from Chicago," Kolberg said. "I've got news for you. It's pouring rain and John drew post twelve."

"Thanks a lot," McAnally said disgustedly. It would now be a long flight to Chicago, as he contemplated the unfortunate turn of events. He had always tried to avoid running John on very bad turf courses, but there was no avoiding this one, not with the whole world watching and Horse of the Year honors hovering over his head.

When he arrived, his worst fears were realized. The

turf course was extremely soft, and with John having to break from the far outside, there was little doubt the horse was going to have a lot to overcome.

Arlington had surrounded the inaugural Million with great pageantry, including parties, black-tie affairs, steeplechase races, show jumping in the infield, Lippizaner stallions, and the playing of the American, English, French, and Irish national anthems.

The McAnallys and the Rubins made their way up to their box and waited. Lefty Nickerson showed up from New York, and even Bubba Snowden came to see his old friend make history. Cenicola and Mercado found a spot by the rail, right on the finish line.

McAnally and Nickerson had conferred in the paddock and agreed that John should be kept off the pace, which promised to be testing over the waterlogged course. Shoemaker allowed John to get his stride and slowly worked his way into position from the far outside, settling in eighth, along the inside. On the front end, Key to Content was being pressed by 40-1 shot The Bart, a tough, consistent stakes horse, trained in Southern California by John Sullivan and ridden by Eddie Delahoussaye.

As they came by the stands and headed into the back-stretch, McAnally knew that John was in trouble. He did-n't say anything to the Rubins, but he could tell watching John's head that there was no rhythm to his stride. When John got into his rhythm, his head would move up and down in perfect cadence with his stride. Shoemaker also could tell John wasn't handling the course, and he just left him alone, gently nudging him along.

As the field approached the half-mile pole, a rush came over McAnally. He could see that familiar head bob. John finally was starting to find his rhythm, as those smooth, daisy-cutting strides began to reappear. But he still had six lengths to make up at the head of the stretch. The Bart, surprisingly, had gotten the better of Key to Content and kicked for home. The crowd went wild as John charged relentlessly down the stretch with his ears pinned back. But The Bart was not coming back to him. John would have to dig down for everything he had. Track announcer Phil Georgeff bellowed, "And John Henry is charging!" As they neared the finish line, everyone knew it was going to come down to a head bob. Both horses took one final lunge, and although John's head was coming down as they hit the wire, it still was too close to call. But the angle of the NBC camera seemed to indicate that The Bart had held on.

Delahoussaye thought John Henry had nipped him, but as they were pulling up, Shoemaker yelled over to him, "I think you beat me." Rubin felt it was a dead-heat, then heard people around him calling The Bart the winner. Cenicola, standing right on the finish line, felt John had gotten his head down in time. NBC's camera angle, however, showed that The Bart was the winner, and they posted the unofficial result on television for the whole world to see. Even The Bart's owner, Franklin Groves, and his wife thought they had won, and rushed down to the winner's circle. Rubin, fearing an uncomfortable situation, decided to remain in his box until it was official.

Finally, the suspense was over, as John Henry's number went up, much to the shock and embarrassment of NBC. As the Rubins and McAnallys made their way down to the winner's circle, they saw The Bart's owners coming back. "When I saw them crying, it took all the guts out of me," Rubin said. "I could see how badly they felt. I, too, had tears in my eyes, for them. But that's horse racing."

Tears also could have been shed for the two courageous Thoroughbreds who had just pushed themselves to the limit. Arlington Park officials could not have written a better script. The great John Henry had shown what champions are made of, and the Arlington Million was on its way to becoming one of the world's most prestigious events. That indelible moment in racing history when John Henry and The Bart hit the wire together lives on in Edwin Bogucki's dramatic statue that overlooks the Arlington Park paddock. It was unveiled in 1989, with the then 14-year-old John Henry and 13-year-old The Bart being paraded in front of the stands in a heartwarming tribute to two gallant horses.

Following the race, while being interviewd by NBC, McAnally kept his promise to Robbins. "There's a guy named Jack in California I'd like to thank for making it possible for us to be here," he said. No sense mentioning his name or profession and putting ideas in people's heads, McAnally thought. Robbins wasn't even aware McAnally had thanked him. He was out playing golf during the race.

If there still were any doubts in anyone's mind that John Henry was Horse of the Year, McAnally decided to eliminate them by sending the horse to Belmont Park for the Jockey Club Gold Cup. John had already won the biggest race on dirt in California and the richest grass race in America. He had won a major weight-for-age grass race in New York, and all that was left was to win the most prestigious weight-for-age dirt race in New York.

But John's herculean effort in the Arlington Million had taken a lot out of him. He lost seventy-five pounds, which is a lot of weight for such a small horse. After being paraded in front of the fans at Del Mar, John began training for the $500,000 Gold Cup. McAnally was familiar enough with the Belmont surface, known as "Big Sandy," to realize that John would have his work cut out for him again. When Belmont is deep and cuppy, it makes the Hollywood dirt track, over which John had finished fourth in the Gold Cup, look like a speedway.

Several days before the Gold Cup John and his faithful crew hopped on a plane yet again and headed back to New York. Awaiting the California invader were Temperence Hill, who had defeated John in the previous year's Gold Cup; Noble Nashua, winner of the Marlboro Cup; Summing, winner of the Belmont

Stakes; and that year's eventual older filly and mare champion Relaxing.

After the break Shoemaker settled John in right behind the leaders and looked to be well in control throughout the mile and a half race. Summing made the same early move that won him the Belmont and disposed of the leaders nearing the head of the stretch. John had moved up steadily from fifth and was ready to strike. Once Shoemaker set him down, he roared by Summing and opened a one and a half-length lead at the eighth pole. Relaxing put in a big move from tenth to second, but that was as close as she could get. Just when the race looked all but over, here came the late charge of 50-1 Peat Moss, another six-year-old gelding. The distance-loving Peat Moss chopped into John Henry's lead from the inside, and Shoemaker had to reach back and ask John for more. The two old geldings charged to the wire, with John holding on to win by a head.

There was no one left to challenge him for Horse of the Year. McAnally and Rubin could have easily put him away for the year, but John returned to California looking for more action, and there was no reason to pass up the rich Oak Tree Invitational. John was 2-5, despite the presence of Spence Bay, winner of four major turf stakes that year, and The Bart, who was coming off an easy victory in the Tanforan Handicap at Bay Meadows and looking for revenge. The move almost backfired. John took on The Bart early and this time put him away with ease. He continued to lead into the stretch, but Spence Bay came charging out of the pack and stuck his neck in front passing the eighth pole. John was in for yet another battle, but this time he looked to be in serious trouble against a top-class horse who apparently had already gotten the better of him. Had they gone to the well once too often? It sure looked that way, until John fought back to win by a neck in a sharp 2:23 2/5 for the mile and a half.

That would have been it for John, if it weren't for the inaugural running of the $500,000 Hollywood Turf Cup on December 6. Running under the lights for the first time, John began to wash out leaving the paddock. He never showed that competitive spark and ran like a tired horse, finishing fourth, beaten two lengths. McAnally was just happy he came out of the race in good shape. He decided to get John away from the racetrack for a freshening and change of scenery and sent him to Galway Downs training center, located in the desert, about sixty miles from Los Angeles.

John had completed one of the most memorable campaigns in racing history. At the Eclipse Awards ceremonies he accounted for a remarkable seven awards: Horse of the Year, champion grass horse, champion older horse, leading owner for Sam Rubin, leading trainer for Ron McAnally, leading jockey for Bill Shoemaker, and leading breeder for Golden Chance Farm. "That was a night above and beyond anything I could have ever dreamed of," Rubin said.

John Henry was now a true superstar in every sense of the word. But it was far from over. Immortality still awaited.

JOHN HENRY

CHAPTER 10

Derailed On The Orient Express

At the ripe old age of seven, John Henry had become a rock star. At least that's the way Lewis Cenicola described him. "It was like he had his own groupies," he said. "Everywhere we went, exercise girls and other girls would come by the barn and just want to touch him or get a piece of his mane. They'd come with all kinds of treats and ask if they could give him something."

But John, whom Cenicola now dubbed "Pappy," still was far from a lovable pet. "He was real ornery as hell," Dr. Robbins said. "He actually was okay once you caught him, but he was a hard catch in his stall. He liked to bare his teeth at you."

Rubin witnessed that firsthand one day at Belmont Park. John would stand in the corner of his stall, behind his hay rack where no one could see him. When Rubin came to visit him, he looked in John's stall and his first thought was that someone had stolen him. He stuck his head in farther and John came charging out of the corner, sending Rubin tumbling backward onto the shedrow floor. He said he remembered seeing nothing but teeth.

Rubin never stopped having fun with his miracle horse. One time he actually threw a bar mitzvah party for John at the Club El Morocco on 53rd Street off Second Avenue in New York City. He invited 150 people and set up a large tote board. Two men dressed as a horse and holding a John Henry sign greeted guests and escorted them inside. Oat bags were hung on the elevators, and finally, a "bar mitzvah" was held for the horse.

John's seven-year-old campaign would begin with fireworks and flares, then crumble in the wake of an injury, finally ending in near tragedy on the other side of the world.

After John returned from Galway Downs, McAnally began plotting strategy. If he followed the previous years' schedule of running in the smaller handicaps, he knew John would have the weight piled on early. This was the Horse of the Year, and races like the San Luis Obispo and San Marcos weren't that attractive or important anymore. It was time to think big, and that meant the Santa Anita Handicap. Rather than start off in a prep, McAnally was confident he could train him up to the race.

Running in the mile and a quarter Big 'Cap cold off a three-month layoff was not something most trainers would have tackled. John had two things going against him. No horse had ever won the Big 'Cap more than once, and only one horse had ever won it without a prep race. That was Cougar II, who was trained by the master, Charlie Whittingham.

McAnally gave John a series of long, solid works to get him fit and sharp for the task ahead. The Saturday before the Big 'Cap he scheduled a mile and an eighth work, but that morning, the skies opened up and turned the Santa Anita surface into a sea of slop. As was the practice following torrential rains, the track was closed to training. McAnally knew he had to get this work into John if the horse were to have any chance of making the race, so he arranged with Santa Anita officials to open the track at eleven o'clock that morning in order for John to work.

McAnally and Cenicola went to the track kitchen for some breakfast and just waited. By eleven, the rain had let

up, and it was time for John to work. He took hold of the track fine and turned in a solid nine furlongs in 1:50 flat.

If McAnally hoped to get a break in the weights by putting John in the Big 'Cap without a prep, it didn't work, as the gelding was assigned top weight of 130 pounds. Each year all major Southern California stakes went through Charlie Whittingham, the dominant force among West Coast trainers for decades. John Henry had humbled Whittingham numerous times already, but the trainer, sensing that John might be vulnerable, threw the kitchen sink in against him. The most formidable Whittingham challenger looked to be Providential II, who had won the previous fall's Washington, D.C., International before defeating John Henry in the Hollywood Turf Cup. Perrault, like Providential, was a top-class horse, but unproven on the dirt. Finally, there was High Counsel, coming off a third in the San Antonio.

A tremendous crowd of 72,752 came to see their hero, and sent John off as the 6-5 favorite. Second choice went to the Laz Barrera-trained It's the One, who was coming off a four-length triumph in the Charles H. Strub Stakes. Adding an element of melodrama to the race was the fact that Perrault would be ridden by Laffit Pincay, who climbed aboard his mount with revenge oozing out of his pores. He had been deeply hurt being taken off John Henry, and although he had nothing against the horse, he would love nothing more than to stick it to Rubin.

At the start, long shot Sir Dancer shot to the front and proceeded to set a blistering pace, while opening a four-length lead. Shoemaker took a good hold of John Henry who dropped well off the pace. After a half in :45, John had two horses beaten and was about a dozen lengths off the lead. Pincay kept Perrault in the second tier, within striking range. Nearing the far turn, Shoemaker had John Henry in gear, and they moved up right behind Perrault as the field began to bunch. It's the One was the first to go after Sir Dancer. John Henry and Perrault moved as a team after the leaders, and, turning for home, the battle was on.

It's the One began to weaken slightly, leaving Perrault and John Henry to slug it out. Pincay, one of the strongest riders in the country, kept pushing hard with those powerful hands and arms, as Shoemaker went to a series of right-handed whips on John Henry. Perrault seemed to be getting the better of John, but when

Pincay saw that familiar white shadow roll back along-
side him on even terms, he pasted Perrault with a brief
but rapid succession of left-handed whips. Both horses
were locked together as they neared the wire, but
Perrault was drifting out badly and shoving John Henry
well out to the middle of the track. Pincay put his whip
away and went back to strong hand urging. John never
backed down, and despite being mugged through the
final sixteenth, he and Perrault hit the wire together.
The photo showed Perrault had won by a nose, but it
didn't take long for the inquiry sign to go up.

And it didn't take long for Perrault to come down. It
was an incredible finish, with both horses crossing the
finish line in 1:59 flat. But, in the end, the best horse
was awarded the victory. To demonstrate what kind of
horse John Henry had defeated, Perrault went on that
year to win the Hollywood Gold Cup on the dirt and
the Arlington Million on the grass.

"Even the owners of Perrault knew he was coming
down when they watched the replay," McAnally said.
"Pincay really wanted to beat John Henry that day.
Watching the race again, it looked to me like there may
have been some revenge in his heart. I've never seen

him hit a horse so quickly in such a short space."

In the winner's circle, Rubin, who was always good for a one-liner, said, "This horse is getting so smart that one of these days he's going to ask me what I'm doing with all his money."

So, John Henry had returned with a vengeance, and McAnally had pulled off one of the sport's greatest training feats. The legendary Calumet Farm trainer H.A. "Jimmy" Jones once called the Santa Anita Handicap "America's toughest race to win." An $1,100 yearling had now done it twice in a row.

But as spring blossomed, the promise of another championship season for John Henry faded. Three weeks after the Big 'Cap, Perrault came back and handed him a sound beating in the San Luis Rey Stakes at equal weights. This clearly was not the real John Henry.

The reason for his uncharacteristic performance was quickly discovered when Dr. Robbins found some calcification around the right front ankle, which John had wrenched during the running of the race. When X-rays taken in early June came back perfect, McAnally began to schedule a training program that would have the horse back jogging and galloping by the first week in July. John was sidelined for almost seven months, and by the time he made it back for the Carleton F. Burke Handicap, it was already October 17, and the year was all but shot.

John ran well in the Burke under 129 pounds, but he seemed rusty from the layoff. He finished fourth, beaten only a length and a half by the top-class Mehmet, who was in receipt of twelve pounds. That race set John up perfectly for the Oak Tree Invitational, which he won easily by two and a half lengths.

The race can best be described by jockey Ray Sibille, who rode runner-up Craelius. The next morning at Santa Anita's Clocker's Corner, Sibille, who was a stutterer, had everyone in stitches as he described the stretch run. "I thought I had it won," he said. "Then I looked over my sh-shoulder and saw that sh-sheepskin noseband coming, and I said to myself, 'Oh, sh-shit!' "

It was now November, and there was little left for John. Rubin, who had done a lot of business with Japanese interests over the years, received an invitation to run in the rich Japan Cup, a one and a half-mile turf race that had been inaugurated the previous year. "I had made a lot of friends there over the years, and I wanted them to see my horse," Rubin said.

McAnally understood that this race was special to Rubin and didn't attempt to talk him out of it. But Marje Everett, vice chairman of the board and chief operating officer of Hollywood Park, was always one to speak her mind, and she warned Rubin about the possible repercussions of such an arduous trip.

"Sam, don't send this horse to Japan," she pleaded. "He's too old. If he were three or four, okay, but not a horse his age."

But Rubin was determined to go, and he accepted the invitation. He would later be sorry he did not heed Everett's words. "She was a hundred percent right," he said. "It was a big mistake to send him."

At first, all seemed wonderful. The Japan Racing Association took care of all the transportation for the Rubins and McAnallys, as well as for Dr. Robbins and his wife, and provided them with suites. "It was first-class treatment all the way," McAnally said. "They treated us like royalty."

But before the royal treatment came the nightmare Lewis Cenicola had to suffer through. Cenicola and Mercado had accompanied John across the country to New Jersey, where he was to run in the Meadowlands

Cup, only fifteen days before the Japan Cup. Once again under the lights, John turned in a dull effort over the Meadowlands dirt track. Carrying top weight of 129 pounds, he ran evenly throughout the mile and a quarter, finishing a non-threatening third behind Mehmet, who this time was getting eleven pounds from John.

After the race Cenicola and Mercado had to scramble to get John to Kennedy Airport. He had to spend a few hours in quarantine there before boarding the plane to Tokyo, which meant leaving Meadowlands by four o'clock that morning. It was an hour van ride to the airport, giving John just the necessary time in quarantine to catch his flight. But when they arrived at Kennedy, they found out the plane had been delayed. Then came another two-hour delay due to a door malfunction. All this time John had to wait, cooped up in a stall barely larger than he was.

When the cargo crew finally began loading, they decided to load John first. Cenicola explained to them that if John was loaded first, he would have to be unloaded last, which meant remaining on the plane until all the other equine passengers were off. He was not about to allow John to get stirred up after such a long flight. So, John was loaded last, and off they went on the biggest adventure of their lives. The plane had to make a stop in Anchorage, Alaska. But after the eight-hour flight, another problem arose, and they wound up sitting on the runway for four hours waiting to take off. When John finally landed in Tokyo, he had lost a day and had been awake for twenty-five straight hours.

Cenicola gave him two days of walking and jogging, then began galloping him. During the gallop, he heard John give a little nicker, something he had never done before. Cenicola had a feeling something wasn't right. He brought John back to the barn and started to wash him down. John never moved. In an instant, he began cramping up, a condition known as tying up. For the next two and a half hours, he stood in that one spot as the sweat poured off him. Cenicola could see he was in pain. He tried to get him to move, but John wouldn't budge. "It was like he was frozen there," Cenicola said.

Finally, John began to move a little, and Cenicola brought him into his stall. One of the Japanese veterinarians tried to get John to lie down in the stall, thinking he had colic. Cenicola knew it wasn't colic, because John had tied up a little in the past. But when the vet got John to lie down, Cenicola grew angry. He couldn't understand

why a vet would let a horse go down with colic. John started to roll around and then suddenly just stopped.

"He didn't move or make a sound for thirty seconds," Cenicola recalled. "I thought he was gone. Then, just like that, he jumped up. When he urinated, it was almost a purplish color."

Cenicola then had to make the unpleasant call to McAnally to let him know what was happening. The vets performed acupuncture on John, and in no time, he was back to normal. When McAnally arrived a couple of days later, John seemed perfect physically and was eating fine, although Robbins told Rubin the horse didn't look quite right. After discussing the situation with McAnally, Rubin decided to run him.

"I should have scratched him," Rubin said. "But I was so impressed with the fact that I owned John Henry, I wanted to show him off to my friends. He checked out physically, and with all the expense they went to bring us all there, I didn't have the heart to scratch him. I assume all the blame. I let my ego get in the way."

Although John was fine physically, everything caught up with him once the race began and he basically loped around the course, finishing thirteenth as the 4-5 favorite. The ordeal had taken its toll, and John returned home a spent horse. He would not make it back to the races until the following July.

McAnally had hoped to make the Santa Anita Handicap, but, instead, he would have to face another crisis. On the morning of February 12, as John was walking off the track following a workout, McAnally noticed the horse was dragging his hind leg. "All I could think was, 'Oh, God, I hope it isn't anything serious,' " he said. "When they're off behind like that, you just pray it's not a fractured pelvis, which is usually fatal."

John returned to his stall and lay down, but was in no distress. McAnally didn't have a clue what was wrong with him and decided to just let him lie there and wait to see what happened. John was such an intelligent horse, he knew how to take care of himself, and he stayed down the remainder of the day. The following morning, McAnally drove up to the barn with all kinds of foreboding thoughts running through his mind. John's stall was right next to the barn entrance, and McAnally could see him standing at the webbing, contentedly munching on hay. "I was never so happy and relieved in all my life," he said.

Dr. Robbins and several other vets determined that John had pulled a muscle in his hip. McAnally brought in a physical therapist who handled National Football League players and other professional athletes. The therapist used a vibrating machine and ultrasound, and applied various solutions to John's hip. Despite the treatment, the injury was slow to heal, and McAnally couldn't even work him for three months.

During this time, speculation grew that perhaps John Henry had seen his best days. He was now eight years old and was coming off an abbreviated campaign, in which he had won only two of six starts. He had amassed $3,609,197 in total earnings, breaking Spectacular Bid's record by over $800,000. There didn't seem to be anything more for him to prove.

But John was far from finished. He still had more spunk than horses half his age, and the fire of competition still burned in those big, bright eyes. When he finally returned in the summer of 1983, however, a major change would be awaiting him. Despite the lofty status he had attained among the greats of the sport, John Henry once again was about to face rejection.

JOHN HENRY

CHAPTER 11

Eight Is Not Enough

The winter and spring of 1983 passed quietly. The Santa Anita meeting, so alive the past three years, just seemed to trudge along without John Henry. Relatively unfamiliar names like Bates Motel, Marfa, Erins Isle, Swing Till Dawn, and Marimbula accounted for the major stakes. John Henry was now eight years old, and the aura of invincibility he had once projected was beginning to fade. In a span of nineteen months, from December 6, 1981, to the end of June, 1983, John had only seen action in three of those months.

The Hollywood Park meeting saw a new star emerge on the scene. A five-year-old French-bred named The Wonder, who had won only two of nine starts in 1982, began thrilling California racing fans with his incredible stretch runs. Trained by Charlie Whittingham, he had come from the clouds to win the San Bernardino

Handicap at Santa Anita on the dirt, the Century Handicap at Hollywood on the grass, and the Californian Stakes at Hollywood on the dirt. He had appeared virtually out of nowhere, and it was anyone's guess just how good this horse was. There was even talk about him becoming John Henry's successor.

The rapid success of The Wonder brought up an intriguing predicament. The five-year-old was ridden by Bill Shoemaker, who went back a long way with Whittingham, riding the majority of his best horses. Defeating The Bald Eagle, as Shoemaker had done so often aboard John Henry, went against the natural order of things in Southern California. Still, it was assumed that once John returned, The Shoe would get back on his old friend.

But with John now eight and on the sidelines for so long, Shoemaker felt it was in his best interests to look to the future and stick with his bread-and-butter trainer. John had been training well and seemingly had bounced back from his ordeal. McAnally was looking at the July 4 American Handicap as John's comeback race and never even gave the jockey situation a second thought. The Shoe had become a part of John Henry, and there was no reason to think this was not a marriage for life.

As the American Handicap approached, Vince DeGregory, who was handling Shoemaker's book while the jockey's regular agent Harry Silbert recuperated from heart surgery, came over to McAnally's barn and told him that Shoemaker and Charlie were old friends, and he was riding all his top horses, including The Wonder. McAnally refused to believe that Shoemaker would desert John Henry and wanted to hear it from Shoe himself.

A week before the race McAnally went to the paddock before a race in which Shoemaker was riding and waited for him to show up.

"Bill, you gonna take off the old horse?" McAnally asked him bluntly.

"Well, I've ridden for Charlie for a long time, and this horse has won three straight stakes," Shoemaker explained.

McAnally tried to plead his case. "Yeah, but the old horse knows you," he said. Shoemaker told him there were a lot of good riders out there who were available, but McAnally gave it one last try. "I know that, but I'd still rather have you."

But Shoemaker held firm and stayed with The Wonder and Whittingham. "I didn't want to lose John

Henry," he said. "But the fact that The Wonder was trained by Charlie had a lot to do with it. I had been riding a lot of good horses for him, and Charlie didn't like it when you took off his horses. John Henry was a great old professional racehorse, the most professional I ever rode, and he knew how to run and when to run. All you had to do was just sit there and guide him along. And he had so much charisma; the public just loved him. But I'm surprised he held up as long as he did. McAnally really did a great job with him."

McAnally had no choice but to accept Shoemaker's decision, and he set out to find a replacement. It didn't take him long to come up with Chris McCarron.

McCarron had developed into one of the best young jockeys in the country after arriving in California in 1978 from Maryland, where he had won an Eclipse Award as leading apprentice rider and set a single-season record for victories with 546 in 1974. After coming to Southern California, he led the nation in money won in 1980 and 1981, and earned his second Eclipse Award in 1980. Although he had won a number of big races, he still hadn't landed that one special horse.

John Henry, meanwhile, had been going through

some sort of minor mid-life crisis. Workouts were beginning to bore him, and he'd just go out there and go through the motions. The action was in the afternoon, when he could grit those teeth and get down to some serious running. But he hadn't been able to do much of that in the past two years. It was as if he had come to realize that mere workouts were accomplishing nothing. To him, it was all work and no play. It became harder and harder for McAnally to get a good work in him. So, he did the only logical thing: he worked John in the afternoon. "The only way he would put out is if he thought he was going out there to race," McAnally said.

John desperately needed a big work before the one and an eighth-mile American Handicap. He was going to have to go into battle against The Wonder and his old rider off a seven-month layoff. McAnally scheduled a mile work on the grass between races with McCarron up. This would be McCarron's first time aboard John, and he wasn't quite prepared for what followed. McAnally told McCarron just to let the horse do what he wanted to. What John wanted to do was blaze a mile over the Hollywood turf in 1:35 flat. "I was in awe,"

McCarron said. "I couldn't believe he worked that fast. And he had such an incredibly smooth, efficient stride."

"I knew Shoemaker watched the work on the monitor in the jocks' room," McAnally said, "and I'm sure he was biting his tongue. He knew after seeing that work that he had made a mistake."

Before the American Handicap McAnally filled McCarron in on what to expect on his first journey aboard John Henry. "John will do anything you want him to," McAnally said. "He'll come off the pace or go to the front, but the best way to beat a closer like The Wonder is to play his game. Just lay back there near him, and when he gets ready to move, you just move right with him." But with a :49 half, and three-quarters in 1:13, McCarron would have had to take a double stranglehold on John to keep him anywhere near The Wonder. He settled him in third, about four or five lengths off the pace, then asked him to turn it on at the head of the stretch.

If McAnally felt Shoemaker regretted his decision to take off John after watching his work, imagine what he thought after the race. John, who was the second-choice behind The Wonder, drew clear in the final furlong to win by a length and a quarter under 127 pounds, closing his final eighth in a sizzling :11 3/5. And what of The Wonder? He finished a lackluster seventh, then after several more dismal races, faded into obscurity.

"Can you imagine, John Henry worked a mile in 1:35, then ran his mile in 1:36 3/5," McCarron said. "You very rarely see a horse work over a full second faster than he runs."

Just like that John Henry was back, and just in time for another crack at the Arlington Million. Once again it looked like he had Charlie Whittingham to beat. Whittingham had Erins Isle, winner of the San Juan Capistrano and Hollywood Invitational, and The Wonder back for another try. From the East came Majesty's Prince, who had knocked off Erins Isle in the Sword Dancer Stakes, and Nijinsky's Secret, a multiple stakes winner who liked to mix it up near the lead.

Once again the Arlington course was wet and deep after recent rains, but at least not as boggy as John's first Million. McAnally knew that Nijinsky's Secret would most likely be the horse John would have to lock horns with first, and he was aware of the horse's tendency to drift out after turning for home.

"If possible, try to get to the inside of this horse," McAnally told McCarron before the race. "This way, if he runs out, he won't carry you with him."

McAnally had the scenario figured out perfectly, but with John breaking from post thirteen and Nijinsky's Secret setting the pace along the rail the whole way, McCarron never got the opportunity to go inside him. Sure enough, when John swung out to challenge for the lead, he got hung up outside Nijinsky's Secret. McCarron set him down hard and he finally stuck his head in front inside the eighth pole. But coming up the inside, through the gap left by Nijinsky's Secret, was the English invader Tolomeo, under a slashing Pat Eddery. Tolomeo, although 38-1, was no slouch, having finished second in the English Two Thousand Guineas and third, beaten a neck, in the Coral-Eclipse Stakes.

McCarron could feel John decelerate slightly after sticking his head in front. But when he saw Tolomeo suddenly appear inside Nijinsky's Secret, he shifted gears and accelerated again. It was too late, however, as Tolomeo hit the wire a neck in front.

As he had done after his 1981 Arlington Million victory, John headed to New York for the Jockey Club

Gold Cup, only to turn in a dull performance, finishing an even fifth behind the easy winner Slew o' Gold.

"Even though John Henry won on the dirt, he really wasn't the same horse as he was on the grass," McCarron said. "He didn't have the same action. He handled the Santa Anita track the best, because it was packed much tighter than the looser, sandier surface at Belmont."

The most significant aspect of the Gold Cup was that the New York Racing Association, to raise funds for the Thoroughbred Retirement Foundation, arranged to bring the three grand old geldings — Kelso, Forego, and John Henry — together on one track. McAnally felt it was a major risk subjecting Kelso, at age twenty-six, to such a stressful undertaking, especially considering the horse hadn't been ridden for fourteen years. The day following the Gold Cup, Kelso was stricken with what was believed to be colic, and he died at 7 p.m. that evening.

John Henry returned to California for his usual appearance in the Oak Tree Invitational. After getting shuffled back from third to seventh, he made a long, sustained move to get the lead inside the sixteenth pole. He appeared to have the race won, but the French filly

Zalataia, a winner over the boys in the Grand Prix de Deauville and La Coupe, came charging late and just got up in the final strides to win by a half-length. It was one of the rare times John had been passed in the stretch. "That was the only way to beat him," McAnally said. "She came from out of the clouds and timed it just right, sneaking up on him at the wire."

After the race Zalataia was sold to Allen Paulson for $2 million and turned over to none other than Ron McAnally. Paulson was getting into the sport on a large scale, and McAnally had the majority of his horses. Paulson wanted to hire McAnally as his private trainer, but with Elmendorf Farm and John Henry, as well as his other clients, McAnally refused the offer.

"Zalataia had been for sale before, but couldn't pass the vet's test," McAnally said. "When Mr. Paulson had her vetted, however, she came through fine, and he made the deal. He really wanted to beat John Henry, and told me, 'We got to buy that filly.' "

The December 11 Hollywood Turf Cup was John Henry's final stop in 1983, and here was McAnally, desperate to have John close out the year on a winning note, challenging him with the filly who had just beaten him and who was now worth $2 million. "I really wasn't nervous about running the two of them together," McAnally said. "I knew John could handle her. She was lucky to have beaten him the first time."

French jockey Freddy Head, who had ridden Zalataia in all her victories, was back on for the Turf Cup. Third choice was the grade I-winning mare Sangue, who was riding a five-race winning streak. Also in the field was Majesty's Prince, who had won the Man o' War Stakes at Belmont Park that fall before finishing third twice to eventual Horse of the Year All Along.

Charlie Whittingham had four in the Turf Cup, and his pacesetter, Prince Florimund, took them on a merry chase for almost a mile over the wet course, labeled good. John Henry tracked him in second, with Zalataia much closer this time in third. Heading into the far turn, John Henry moved up to take a slight lead, with Zalataia just off his flank and Sangue charging up on their outside. Sangue then stuck her head in front nearing the head of the stretch and the three-way battle was on. John had to fight hard, but finally wore down Sangue inside the sixteenth pole, and just as he did, Zalataia came flying on his outside in an attempt

to snatch victory from the old boy once again. But John was still in full battle mode and wasn't about to be caught napping this time. He held off Zalataia to win by a half-length.

That victory was enough to earn John Henry another Eclipse Award for male turf horse. For the first time since 1980, John would be going into the new year off a victory, giving Rubin and Team McAnally hope that, despite all the miles and wear and tear, the big train was still far from the end of the line. Although 1984 wouldn't start off the way they'd hoped, it would turn out to be a year to remember. And when it was over, John Henry would be acclaimed as one of the true marvels in the annals of sport.

JOHN HENRY

CHAPTER 12

Closing Night

It was 8:45 on the morning of March 4, 1984, and the peaks of the San Gabriel mountains already were piercing a bright cerulean sky. Temperatures were supposed to reach no higher than the mid-seventies, and everything looked perfect for the big day ahead.

Outside the gates of Santa Anita, people already were gathering. The anticipation grew as the nine o'clock opening approached. It was like Dorothy and company awaiting entrance into Emerald City. In this Oz, however, it was a racetrack grandstand that was adorned in green, and the wizard was a four-legged, ageless enchanter named John Henry.

That afternoon the nine-year-old phenomenon would attempt to perform another of his wondrous feats of magic by winning the Santa Anita Handicap for the third time. By noon the parking lots were full as thousands of picnickers found their spot in the infield. Soon the grandstand and apron were a mass of humanity.

John Henry's name was plastered all over the newspapers, and the vacancy signs outside the local motels now read, "Good Luck, John Henry." By the time the crowd had finished settling in, 74,687 fans had amassed, the third-largest crowd in Santa Anita history. The last time the track had seen a larger crowd was back in 1947.

As John walked around the paddock before the race, he was greeted by waves of applause and the constant clicking of cameras. Sent off as the 2-1 favorite, his main threats looked to be Interco, winner of the San Fernando Stakes, and the San Antonio winner Poley. The crowd let out a cheer when track announcer Dave Johnson called John moving from seventh to fourth on the far turn. But instead of building into a glorious crescendo, the cheers faded into silence, as John struggled home in fifth, well behind the victorious Interco.

John came out of the Big 'Cap a tired horse, and once again came the speculation that he finally was nearing the end. That speculation escalated after John was beaten by Interco again in the San Luis Rey, but this time John had fought hard on the lead most of the way, finishing a gutsy third, only three-quarters of a length behind the winner.

McAnally decided to change course and ship John up to Golden Gate Fields for the Golden Gate Handicap as a confidence builder. So, while Interco was winning again, this time in the Century Handicap at Hollywood, John was up north the same day, having an easy time with five outclassed rivals. Sent off at 1-2, he defeated the improving Silveyville by two lengths, and his time of 2:13 for the mile and three-eighths took three-fifths of a second off the course record.

John's next stop was the Hollywood Invitational, a race he had won in 1980 and 1981. Interco's trainer Ted West decided to pass and await the Californian Stakes on the dirt. But John still would have his hands full with San Juan Capistrano winner Load the Cannons, one of three Charlie Whittingham-trained horses. No one can say Whittingham didn't go after John Henry with all cylinders loaded.

After moving his stable from Santa Anita to Hollywood, McAnally noticed that John's training picked up. He hadn't taken to the Santa Anita track as well as he had in the past, and McAnally had to work him in company to get him to extend himself. Before the Hollywood Invitational, John worked a mile by himself in 1:38, the fastest work on the tab for the distance.

John drew the rail and was stuck down on the inside for the entire race. Chris McCarron, surrounded by all three Whittingham horses, waited patiently for a hole. When he found one, John blasted through with a quick burst. Two of Whittingham's horses went into retreat, including Load the Cannons, but the third, Galant Vert, was charging on the outside and looking very strong, sticking his neck in front inside the eighth pole. John battled back courageously and began reaching out with those graceful, powerful strides. With his neck fully outstretched, he crossed the wire a half-length in front in stakes-record time. At age nine, the victories and the earnings were still piling up, and he was still breaking track and stakes records. John Henry had won his thirty-fifth race and pushed his earnings over the $4.7-million mark.

The day before John won the Golden Gate Handicap, Claiborne Farm's Swale had captured the Kentucky Derby at Churchill Downs, and he would go on to win the Belmont Stakes as well. Except for champion Conquistador Cielo's brief fling with glory in 1982, the three-year-olds of the eighties had not managed to stir the imagination as their immediate predecessors had done. Perhaps Swale would be the one. But on a peaceful spring morning the weekend after the Belmont, as Swale was being washed, he suddenly went down on his hind legs, then flipped over and died. The colt's heart had simply stopped.

The nation was stunned. For the past four years John Henry had carried the load as the sport's only true superstar, and racing fans all over America now turned to him once again in the wake of Swale's death. This had been one of the longest love affairs in memory, comparable to Kelso in the sixties and Forego in the seventies. But Kelso had begun slowing down at age eight, and was retired after a fourth-place finish in an allowance sprint in his only start at nine. Forego, plagued by calcium deposits on his knees, raced only twice at eight before being retired.

McAnally and Rubin now began looking ahead three months at another try in the Arlington Million. Rubin actually had been looking even farther down the road to the first Breeders' Cup, the brainchild of breeder John Gaines, which was scheduled to see the light of day on November 10 at Hollywood Park. NBC agreed to devote four hours to the Breeders' Cup, giving this new racing extravaganza the necessary exposure to become one of the top sporting events in the world. The second richest race of the seven carded was the mile and a half Breeders' Cup Turf, with a purse of $2 million. What a perfect opportunity to showcase John Henry to the entire world.

But, although the race was still five and a half months away, Rubin had already stated emphatically that he was against running John Henry. Because Ole Bob Bowers was not among the 1,035 stallions nominated to the Breeders' Cup, Rubin would have to pay $400,000 to supplement him to the race. With that money going back to Breeders' Cup Ltd. and not to the purse, it meant that Rubin would be putting up $400,000 to win the winner's share of $600,000. That went against Rubin the bettor and businessman. "I told them I'd put up the money if it went back into the pot, but they refused," Rubin said. So, for now, the Breeders' Cup was merely a faint speck off in the distance. There were other races to be won.

One of them was the Hollywood Gold Cup, the race that broke up what would have been a nine-racing winning streak for John back in 1981. Things would be no different this time. John ran an excellent race, sitting just behind the leaders and responding when McCarron called on him turning for home. Although he closed strongly in the final furlong he couldn't overtake Desert Wine, who had just defeated Interco in the Californian Stakes. John had been beaten, but he would never taste defeat again.

Next came the one and a half-mile Sunset Handicap at Hollywood before a return trip to Chicago and the Arlington Million. Needless to say, John once again stumbled upon a nest of Bald Eagle runners, as Whittingham threw four in against him this time — Galant Vert, Load the Cannons, Gato Del Sol, and Craelius — all of whom had seen quite enough of John Henry already. John carried top weight of 126 pounds, but conceded eight to fifteen pounds to his eight opponents.

John ran his typical race, lying back in fourth then moving up steadily into contention. Surprisingly, an 83-1 shot named Pair of Deuces still held a length lead at the eighth pole, but John put him away, then turned

back a brief, but stiff, challenge from Load the Cannons to win by a length in 2:24 4/5, just four-fifths off the course record.

Rubin had once promised John Henry a condominium in Florida when he retired, but after the Sunset, he said John wasn't thinking that small any longer. "Now he's thinking about something in the south of France," Rubin said, with his typical impish grin. Actually, Rubin had already made plans for John's retirement, promising the horse to his friend Joe Taub, who owned Sterlingbrook Farm near Pittstown, New Jersey, just a few miles from the Delaware River.

McAnally began gearing John Henry up for the Arlington Million, giving him several solid works at Del Mar before shipping to Chicago. It was hard to believe it had been three years since his epic battle with The Bart. But McAnally could see little change in the old horse. "He still loved to race and hadn't lost any of his zest for competition," he said.

John arrived in Chicago and immediately took to the turf course, which finally was firm and enabled him to use that smooth stride of his. The morning before the race, he blew out three furlongs and just glided over the turf in :35 2/5. "His action and motion were phenomenal," McCarron said.

John's main competition looked to come from Desert Wine, who had just finished a close third in the Eddie Read Handicap at Del Mar in his turf debut; his old obstacle Nijinsky's Secret, whom he'd likely have to avoid once again turning for home; and the Whittingham-trained Gato Del Sol. Leading French trainer Andre Fabre was represented by the hard-knocking pair of Mourjane and Crystal Glitters. John Gosden had the classy filly Royal Heroine, who had finished first in her previous three starts but was disqualified in her most recent race, the Palomar Handicap at Del Mar. She had also defeated colts, winning the nine-furlong Inglewood Handicap at Hollywood in near-course-record time.

Although it looked as if Nijinsky's Secret would be the likely pacesetter, it was Royal Heroine, under Fernando Toro, who shot out of the one-hole and opened a length lead over Nijinsky's Secret. McCarron had John Henry sitting about two lengths behind while saving ground, with Desert Wine right beside him.

"I was surprised to see Royal Heroine in front,"

McCarron said. "I was comfortable where I was because I knew John was the type of horse who had the ability to get himself out of trouble. He was so agile, he would actually wait and look for a hole himself, then go for it when one opened."

Royal Heroine was able to cut out easy fractions of :48 2/5 and 1:12 2/5. When Nijinsky's Secret came up on her outside to challenge, she had more than enough to turn him away. McCarron had taken John off the rail, and as Nijinsky's Secret moved out, he drove John up between horses and took off after Royal Heroine. "It was tight in there," McCarron said, "but there was no way I was going to go around Nijinsky's Secret again."

The Irish-bred filly held tough to the eighth pole, but John was skipping along so effortlessly over the turf, there never was any doubt about the outcome. He collared Royal Heroine inside the final furlong and quickly drew off to win by a length and three-quarters, blazing his final quarter in :24.

After the race Gosden saw McAnally and said, "What a horse! My mare was in the best shape of her life. She couldn't have been doing any better."

To show just how good a filly Royal Heroine was,

later that year she would knock off the best milers in the world, winning the inaugural Breeders' Cup Mile by a length and a half. Her time of 1:32 3/5 shattered Hollywood's course record by a full second and came within two-fifths of Dr. Fager's world record.

Toro offered no excuses. The reason for Royal Heroine's defeat was pretty clear to him. "She proved she's the best filly in the country," he said. "She just got beat by John Henry." That said it all.

With John Henry on another roll, and now racing's first $5-million earner, the subject again turned to the Breeders' Cup. Rubin stood by his guns. The thought of putting up that much money and not having the opportunity to win it back seemed incomprehensible to him. "You've got to be an idiot of a businessman to do that," he said.

A tentative schedule had already been mapped out for John. The day following the Million, he left for Belmont Park to point for the Turf Classic at a mile and a half. After that, he would either return home for the Oak Tree Invitational or head to Woodbine in Canada for the Rothmans International. Another possibility was the inaugural running of the Ballantine's Scotch Classic at the Meadowlands on October 13.

The Turf Classic turned into a classic showdown between Horses of the Year John Henry and the great French filly All Along. With John having raced only five times in 1983 and missing half the year, All Along became the darling of racing fans in three countries, as she beat the best horses in Europe in the Prix de l'Arc de Triomphe before coming to North America and steamrolling her way to victories in the Rothmans International in Canada, and the Turf Classic and Washington, D.C. International in the United States.

All Along had not run since the D.C. International, but that didn't concern her trainer Patrick-Louis Biancone in the slightest. He was confident his filly was 100 percent ready to take on anyone, and that included John Henry. "He is a very tough horse, but I don't think she can be beaten," Biancone said.

The New York Racing Association stepped up its advertising campaign, releasing a huge ad that showed John Henry in action superimposed against a Wall Street ticker-tape parade. The ad read: "This Saturday at Belmont Park. **John Henry** The greatest winner in history comes to Town. Don't miss this $5 1/2 million Legend on Legs." John Gosden may have been right when he said of John Henry, "He's the greatest thing that ever happened to horse racing."

The Turf Classic's $625,250 purse was the largest in New York history. John Henry was sent off as the even-money favorite, with All Along 9-5. Other top-class horses entered were Majesty's Prince, who had recently won the Man o' War Stakes for the second year in a row, and the Man o' War runner-up Win. As the horses paraded around the walking ring before the race, the New York fans let it be known to whom their hearts belonged, as they gave John a rousing ovation.

At the start, no one seemed willing to act as pacesetter, so McCarron obliged by sending John Henry right to the front, then proceeded to slow the pace down. Tracked by Win, John got away with dawdling fractions of :48 4/5 and 1:13, which all but did in All Along and Majesty's Prince. All Along made a quick move into contention nearing the quarter pole, pulling to within two lengths of John Henry, who was now being challenged by Win. The pair battled the length of the stretch, with the New York-bred Win getting almost on even terms. All Along and Majesty's Prince gave it all they had, but John's final quarter in :23 3/5

sealed their fate. Down to the wire, he dug in determinedly and refused to give in to Win, who was clinging to him like a terrier to a pant leg. John hit the wire a neck in front, and his time of 2:25 1/5 was only two-fifths of a second off Secretariat's course record.

John Henry had won five of his last six starts. Maybe Sam Rubin was right. Maybe John *would* race until his bar mitzvah. Mercado may have called him "El Viejo," Spanish for the Old One, and Cenicola may have dubbed him Pappy, but there certainly was nothing old about John Henry.

Meadowlands was desperate to land John Henry for the Ballantine's Scotch Classic. What better way to start off with a new race and sponsor than to draw the sport's biggest attraction. By running in New York, he was already right there in their own backyard. But the race lacked any prestige, and its $200,000 purse couldn't compete with the $600,000 Rothmans International the following week or even the $400,000 Oak Tree Invitational a week after that. It didn't take a genius to figure out that there was an excellent chance John was going to win the Turf Classic, so Meadowlands put its ante in the pot. A few days before the Turf Classic, management doubled the purse to $400,000 and offered a $500,000 bonus to any horse who could win the Turf Classic and Ballantine's Scotch Classic.

That was a deal Rubin couldn't refuse, and he announced that John Henry would run at the Meadowlands, but insisted he would have run without the bonus. Ironically, the president of Ballantine's was named John Henry Hobbs, and his office was directly across the street from "21," the restaurant that Rubin would frequent occasionally for lunch. "The embarrassing part was that whenever I ran into him after that, I could never remember his name," Rubin said.

A lack of rain that fall had caused the Meadowlands turf course to become rough, drawing criticism from local trainers. The maintenance crew put up a temporary rail to protect the inside of the course and continued to work feverishly on it. Luckily, heavy rains the week before the race helped a great deal, and by the night of the race the course was in relatively good shape.

John was assigned top weight of 126 pounds, which also drew criticism from rival horsemen. Although the actual weight seemed low for a horse of John Henry's stature, Meadowlands racing secretary Eual Wyatt con-

centrated more on the spread, and John had to con-
cede from six to seventeen pounds to his eleven opponents. Back to challenge him again was Win, along
with United Nations Handicap winner Hero's Honor
and Arlington Handicap winner Who's for Dinner.

A crowd of nearly 36,000 showed up to witness history. In the saddling area before the race, McAnally
told McCarron, "It doesn't look as if there's much speed
in there, so try not to let him drop back too far."

Neither McAnally nor Rubin liked the way John
was acting. He was so uncharacteristically docile,
Rubin thought he was sick. Even McAnally said he'd
never seen him like that before.

John Henry and McCarron broke from post four.
McCarron nudged him along, but he didn't grab hold of
the bit like he normally did. By the time they had gone a
quarter of a mile, John had dropped back to eighth, some
ten lengths off the lead. On the front end, Win was mix-
ing it up with Hero's Honor and long shot Gateshead.
Down the backstretch, John still was well out of it, nine
lengths back. "I kept asking him to pick it up," McCarron
said, "but he just wouldn't grab the bit."

Up in the box, no one knew what was happening.

"We didn't know what to think," Rubin said. "We felt maybe it was the lights."

As John lagged back off the pace, Rubin looked at McAnally, seeking some sort of reassurance, but McAnally was just as bewildered. "Maybe we ran him too much this year," Rubin said. No sooner than he had finished the sentence, John suddenly took off heading into the far turn and shot into fifth passing the three-eighths pole. When McCarron swung him to the outside, John looked ready to inhale the foursome in front of him. As they turned for home, Hero's Honor and Win were still at each other, with Who's For Dinner ready to strike. McCarron gave John one right-handed smack of the whip, and in a flash he charged up on the outside, still running on his left lead. Inside the eighth pole, John switched to his right lead and burst clear so quickly, it looked as if the others were running through a bog.

Track announcer Dave Johnson shouted, "And the old man, John Henry, takes command." John's performance inspired *New York Post* columnist Ray Kerrison to write, "John Henry raises goose pimples on the flesh. He is unreal. He is eerie."

The crowd felt the wave of emotion as well and went wild. They knew they were witnessing something extraordinary; something that would become etched in the history books. But what they didn't know was just how profound a moment this was. That image of the ageless John Henry floating effortlessly over the turf on his way to another sensational victory would be a sight never to be seen again. John swept across the finish line two and three-quarters in front of Who's For Dinner, equaling the course record for a mile and three-eighths.

In a few moments he would walk proudly into the winner's circle for the last time.

CHAPTER 13

Saying Goodbye

Sam Rubin had a decision to make. For the past several months, he had provided a very sane and logical reason why he shouldn't run John Henry in the inaugural Breeders' Cup Turf. But he knew as the big event grew closer the pressure would increase.

With a remarkable campaign behind him, in which he had gone over the $6-million mark in earnings, John was right in the thick of things for Horse of the Year honors. In most any other year he would already have had it locked up, but there was a monster back East named Slew o' Gold who had all but annihilated the competition in New York. The son of Seattle Slew had emerged into a major star at the end of 1983 and picked up where he had left off in '84, winning all five of his starts. He had toyed with the top-class Track Barron in the Whitney Handicap at Saratoga in an almost embarrassing display of superiority, then rolled through the Woodward, Marlboro Cup, and Jockey Club Gold Cup. In the Gold Cup, he ran to his 1-10 odds, breezing home by almost ten lengths.

It was going to be a battle to the wire for racing's highest honor, and it likely would come down to the Breeders' Cup. A victory by Slew o' Gold in the Classic would make it difficult to deprive him of Horse of Year. John's only chance would be to close out his campaign with a win in the Turf. Then it would be up to the voters to decide, and John definitely would have sentiment on his side.

The big day grew closer, and John Henry still was a holdout. If he was going to be supplemented, Rubin would have to submit an initial payment of $133,000, which was non-refundable. Just prior to the deadline, Rubin was in California, and he received a phone call in his hotel from Marje Everett, whose words Rubin had not heeded prior to John's ill-fated trip to Japan. Everett knew what having John Henry would do for Hollywood Park and the Breeders' Cup, and she pleaded with Rubin to run the horse. "Hollywood Park had always been very good to us, and she was quite a lady," Rubin said. "I decided the next day to put up the money."

John Henry, however, was having problems. The

grass course had become chewed up toward the end of the Santa Anita meeting, which closed on November 6, four days before the Breeders' Cup. John developed a filling in his left foreleg, which McAnally believed was caused by the condition of the turf. It still looked as if he had a chance to make the big race if they could get the filling down in time.

The day after speaking with Everett, Rubin stopped by McAnally's barn and dropped off a check for $133,000. On the morning of October 30, the day payment was due, the filling was still there. McAnally called Rubin and asked what he should do.

"Sam, there's a question whether we're gonna be able to make it," McAnally said. "He's got this filling and we can't get it out. It's around the suspensory area, right above the ankle. It's not bad, but it's there. I have your check in my hand. What do you want me to do with it?"

Rubin thought about it for a few seconds, then told McAnally, "Take it over to Marje. He's earned it."

So, McAnally drove across town to Hollywood Park and handed Everett the check, knowing full well that there was a good possibility John would not be able to make the race.

The leg never responded to treatment. Dr. Robbins had diagnosed it as a strain of the branch of the suspensory ligament, and there really wasn't much that could be done for it. For an injury such as this, time was the only remedy. Four days after delivering the check, McAnally made the call to Rubin. John Henry was finished for the year.

All that remained now was to see what happened in the Breeders' Cup. It would no doubt take a defeat by Slew o' Gold to keep John in the running for Horse of the Year. In the Turf, the French invader Lashkari hung a neck defeat on All Along at odds of 53-1. Next came the Classic. Slew o' Gold looked so strong that he was sent off at 3-5. But the colt had been suffering from foot problems for a while and developed a quarter crack on his right front hoof. Dr. Judd Butler was called in to patch it, but Slew o' Gold didn't seem comfortable in his works. In the Classic he couldn't get by long shot Wild Again and had to settle for third, beaten a half-length. However, the subsequent disqualification of second-place finisher Gate Dancer moved him up to second. All that was left now was the voting.

If Slew o' Gold had one thing going for him, it was the

fact that he was the meat in the sandwich down the stretch, getting bumped and squeezed from both sides. But many also felt he was a beaten horse well before the rough stuff began.

On February 8, 1985, the Eclipse Awards Dinner was held at the Century Plaza Hotel in Los Angeles. When it came time for the announcement of Horse of the Year, a hush fell over the crowd of 1,400. Unlike most years, this was going to be a nail biter. James E. (Ted) Bassett, president of the Thoroughbred Racing Associations, stepped up to the microphone and opened the envelope. "Like old wine..."

That was as far as he got. A tremendous cheer went up from the crowd, and all at once everyone stood and saluted John with a rousing ovation, as the Rubins and McAnally went up to accept the award. John Henry had become the first nine-year-old ever to be voted Horse of the Year. It wasn't until the following day that everyone became aware that John had won by a single vote. Once again he had emerged victorious in a photo finish.

As John Henry headed into his ten-year-old campaign, the big question was how quickly the suspensory injury would heal. In January the leg was treated

with a blistering agent in an effort to improve circulation and expedite healing, and over the next several months, it began to show steady improvement. McAnally scrutinized John Henry's every move to make sure the old boy still was mentally and physically ready to continue with his career. For Rubin, no news was good news. "As long as he shows us he's still competitive he'll continue to race," Rubin said. "This is what he was born to do. He doesn't know anything else."

During this time the Kentucky Horse Park contacted Rubin in an attempt to get John Henry to live out his days there at the end of his career. Rubin went to the Horse Park, which was home to the great Forego, as well as Rossi Gold, A Letter to Harry, and the Standardbred champion Rambling Willie. He liked what he saw but still felt obligated to honor the commitment he had made to Taub. He told Taub about the Horse Park's offer but said if he still wanted the horse, that's where he'd go. Taub realized that John would be happier with all the activity at the Horse Park, where people could come and visit him, and he released Rubin from his promise.

Later in the spring, John had a minor setback in the

same leg, but it quickly healed. McAnally didn't want to bring John back in a tough spot at his age and risk injuring the leg again, and the Vernon O. Underwood Handicap at Hollywood Park on July 22 looked like an ideal spot. On July 11, John worked a mile on the grass in a sharp 1:36 1/5 and looked like his old self.

But soon after the work Mercado noticed that the area around the suspensory was sensitive to the touch. The troubled leg began to fill again, and Dr. Robbins was called in. "I thought it was the deep flexor tendon," he said, "but when we had it scanned, it showed a high suspensory strain."

As in the past, the tenderness disappeared, and McAnally tested it by galloping John a mile and three-eighths. But when Dr. Robbins examined the leg, the filling was still there.

Hollywood Park prepared for a huge turnout on what promised to be the biggest day of the year. Three days before the race, McAnally called Rubin to tell him the latest situation, and they agreed to scratch the horse. Hollywood officials asked McAnally if John Henry could parade between races the day before the Underwood on Swaps Stakes day. But with a big crowd expected that day as well, McAnally didn't want to take a chance on John getting stirred up and aggravating the injury.

As the weekend approached, the injury still showed no signs of healing. McAnally then made the call to Rubin that he had dreaded for a long time. "Sam, I'm afraid we've come to the end of the line," he said.

For Rubin and McAnally there was a sense of relief. They had been having horrifying visions of John breaking down on the track. McAnally relayed his fears to Rubin before making the announcement to retire the horse. "I'd never be able to forgive myself if they ever had to haul him off the track," McAnally said. Rubin felt the same way. "I think I would have dropped dead if something had happened to him while he was running in a race," he said.

McAnally notified Hollywood Park, which made the official announcement over the public address system one hour before the Swaps Stakes. On the Diamond Vision board in the infield appeared the words: "Hollywood Park Salutes JOHN HENRY Champion of Champions!" Rubin had decided not to attend. He didn't think he and Dorothy could handle it, and instead they took a two-hour walk and just reminisced about all the wonderful times and great thrills they'd had, and how blessed they were to have this remarkable animal come into their lives. He did send a message to the fans, saying in part, "The time has come. He's given us a wonderful life, and he's touched the lives of a lot of people all over the country."

After the stunning news had sunk in, the crowd gave John Henry a warm round of applause, as if to thank him for so many wonderful memories. A week later, in a letter to McAnally that he made public, Rubin said, "This is a personal and public thank you, thank you, thank you. You have been more than a trainer — you have been a dear friend, and truly John Henry grew because of you. You are a true lover of animals, and I have never seen anyone display more feelings for animals than you. Your staff who dedicated themselves to John's well being, too, have earned our respect and admiration. You can now rent the spare room at your home. John will not be coming home on weekends."

McCarron, like everyone else, was saddened by John's retirement. But he felt no one was any sadder than John himself. "He loved to race," he said. "He enjoyed what he was doing and was happy at the racetrack."

Oscar Wilde wrote: "The tragedy of old age is not that one is old, but that one is young." The tragedy of John Henry's retirement was not that a horse had grown too old to race, it was that a horse who still possessed the heart and spirit of a youngster had grown too old to race.

For McAnally, John's retirement would be a major void in his life that he knew would never be filled.

"I just thank God every day of my life that we were given the opportunity to have him," he said. "And just think, it all came about from a phone call from an owner I had never met before. This one horse changed the lives of everyone around him. It's sad that it's over, but it was a great run in the sun."

CHAPTER 14

Out Of Mothballs

After turning John Henry out in his new paddock at the Kentucky Horse Park, Jose Mercado handed the lead shank over to the gelding's new groom, Don Moore. The two men had known each other on the racetrack, which made it a little easier for Mercado, who was asked to stay for two weeks and help Moore and John get acquainted.

At a black-tie dinner on August 30, held outside the Hall of Champions barn, speeches were given by Governor Collins, Rubin, and Keeneland president Ted Bassett, who had announced John Henry's Horse of the Year selection earlier that year. McAnally and Rubin were awarded the honorary rank of Kentucky Colonel by Governor Collins, who had been instrumental in getting John to come to the Horse Park.

Following the festivities and dinner, the dignitaries

made their way into the barn to visit with the guest of honor. The following day, under bright blue skies, 13,000 visitors poured into the Horse Park to celebrate "John Henry Day," which included free admission and a variety of activities. Mercado, who also was made a Kentucky Colonel by Governor Collins at that afternoon's ceremonies, brought John Henry out and walked him in front of his many fans, who cheered their hero, as one loud cry of "Bravo!" resounded from the crowd.

John seemed content in his new home and loved mingling with the crowds each day during his three showings. At 3:45 in the afternoon, after his final show, he was let out in his paddock where he'd run to his heart's content.

But John was still John, and he wanted no intrusions on his private life. Soon after arriving at the Horse Park, he was given a goat named Ba Ba Louie as a companion. After John got through with her, it took two hundred dollars in vet bills to patch her up. The only living creatures he would now tolerate were birds, which he allowed to nest in his stall.

In the early spring of 1986, Keeneland officials arranged with Rubin and the Horse Park to have John paraded in front of the fans at Keeneland. On April 5, 1986, after a little over seven months of blissful retirement, John Henry found himself back at the racetrack. Rubin and McAnally were in attendance, and Rubin could see that old spark still shining in John's eyes. In the paddock, he became unruly, and they had to cut his appearance short for fear he might injure himself. The way Rubin saw it, maybe the fire hadn't been extinguished. Maybe there was enough of a flame left to be rekindled. The seed was planted that John may still have the urge to race, that the magical journey wasn't quite over.

Shortly after John's appearance at Keeneland, Alan Balch, head of marketing at Santa Anita, approached McAnally and Rubin about bringing John Henry to California to parade before the Breeders' Cup crowd. McAnally wasn't crazy about the idea. He felt it would be putting John at great risk to expose him to such an electrically charged atmosphere and a large crowd after such a long time away from the track. He told Rubin if he really wanted to do it, he'd have to bring the horse out there in advance and put him in light training in order to get him used to the racetrack atmosphere. He believed that was the only safe way to go about it.

Rubin thought about John's appearance at Keeneland, and the glory days came rushing back like a tidal wave. He felt if he was going to bring John back and put him in light training anyway, why not see whether it was feasible to race him again. John was examined by veterinarian Dr. Robert Copelan, who pronounced him fit enough to resume training. He then was put on a plane and sent back to McAnally, who never thought he'd ever see John's face peering out of his stall again. The old warrior had returned to his old battleground.

John began slowly, walking for several days and then jogging around the half-mile training track. His muscles clearly were not ready for this regimen, and he almost tied up, as he had done in Japan and on several other occasions. But he soon adapted to the routine, and on May 22, he went to the track for the first time for a gallop with his old buddy Lewis Cenicola aboard. To prevent him from getting too excited, Cenicola brought him on and off the track at the gap midway down the backstretch rather than the more populated main gap.

By early July, John still was about a hundred

pounds overweight, weighing in at 1,100 pounds, compared with his usual 1,000. On July 2, he had his first official breeze, going two furlongs in :24 at Hollywood. Five days later he breezed three furlongs in :36 4/5. Continuing on a five-day work schedule, McAnally sent him out on July 12 for a half-mile breeze and told Cenicola, "Just sit on him and let him do what he wants." John went in :50, and although he seemed to be doing everything the right way, Cenicola said he just didn't feel like the same horse.

"He wasn't as eager, and he didn't get into the bit the way he used to," Cenicola said. "Physically, he looked okay, but he didn't have the same enthusiasm. I'd been around old horses who needed a couple of races after a layoff, so maybe John just needed a race or two to wake him up a little."

It was now almost August, and Arlington Park honed in on John Henry's scent like hound dogs to a drag. They had been after Rubin to get him to run again in the Million, but there wasn't enough time to make the race, so it was agreed that John would parade before the fans on "John Henry Day," two days before the Million.

Meanwhile, the McAnally stable moved down to Del Mar, and John continued his steady training pattern, working on July 30 and August 4. But that was as far as they got. Once again, John developed a filling in his ankle, which was diagnosed as a torn suspensory ligament. McAnally put it plain and simple: "Time has run out."

It was decided to keep him in California for three weeks and then return to the Horse Park. But the original goal of parading on Breeders' Cup Day still was doable, and plans were changed to let him remain with McAnally, then come home after the Breeders' Cup. Meadowlands also wanted to capitalize on the John Henry goodwill tour across America and convinced Rubin that a stop in New Jersey would be the perfect place for John to bid a final farewell to his fans, just as he had done as a racehorse in the Ballantine's Scotch Classic.

In August, back at the Horse Park, John's groom Don Moore quit, and park officials hired twenty-two-year-old Wes Lanter, who had worked as a stallion groom at Spendthrift Farm. Lanter had been a big John Henry fan and had attended classes at the Kentucky Equine Institute at the Horse Park. Kathy Hopkins, who ran the school and was head of equine operations at the Horse Park, told Lanter of the opening, and he jumped at the chance to work with John and Forego.

As the Breeders' Cup approached, McAnally suggested that Lanter come to California for five days and spend time with John Henry so that they could get to know each other. Mercado filled him in on all of John's habits and eccentricities, and the two hit it off right from the start. "He had his little quirks," Lanter said, "but we got along great. Dealing with stallions at Spendthrift, I'd seen a lot worse."

On Breeders' Cup Day, John was brought out following Lady's Secret's Horse of the Year-clinching victory in the Distaff. As Mercado walked him on the track, the stretch calls of John's memorable wins in the first Arlington Million and Ballantine's Scotch Classic blared over the public address system. Up in the stands, an emotional Chris McCarron, who had been injured in a spill and was doing color commentary for NBC, told viewers, "I get goose bumps just hearing those calls again. What an amazing animal he was." After parading at the Breeders' Cup, John, Lanter, and Mercado boarded a plane and headed to New Jersey.

At Newark Airport, Mercado led John down the

ramp and into a two-horse trailer, then once again said goodbye to his long-time friend. "Jose gave John a hug and pat him on the head," Lanter recalled. "As he walked down the ramp to get back on the plane, John looked at him and his ears perked up. Then, he let out this yelp, as if he were really saying goodbye to him. It was really eerie."

John was given his typical rousing ovation at the Meadowlands, as the track presented Rubin and McAnally with a special farewell blanket. Then it was back on a plane to Lexington and the Kentucky Horse Park. "When we got off the van, John looked around and gave a little nicker," Lanter said. "He knew he was home, and he was happy."

JOHN HENRY

EPILOGUE

Living Legend

It was a cool, overcast afternoon, several days before the 1990 Kentucky Derby. Ron McAnally was running his $1,500 bargain-basement yearling Silver Ending, owned by his wife Debbie, in the big race. But no trip to Kentucky would be complete without a visit to the Kentucky Horse Park to see an old and dear friend.

McAnally, carrying a large plastic bag of apples, walked into John Henry's paddock and approached the back door to his stall, which led directly to the paddock. "Hey, you get out here," McAnally said softly, as if speaking to his pet dog. John knew that voice meant treats, and he ambled out the door, looking to see what McAnally had brought him. As John walked up to him, eyeing the bag intently, McAnally continued to speak tenderly to the horse. "Oh, my goodness," he said. "Oh my. Look what I brought you." McAnally took out an apple and fed it to John, looking at the old horse with the same wonderment and admiration as always. "Here you go, Pappy," he said, as he continued to feed him apples.

McAnally realized a few years earlier that John still remembered his voice. The horse was in the far end of his paddock and hadn't seen him. He was too busy staring at a group of Clydesdales pulling a wagon down a nearby road. McAnally figured this would be a good test to see if his voice could overcome John's fascination with the Clydesdales. He called John's name, and the horse turned toward him and threw his ears up. "He let out a big yell and came running down to where I was," McAnally said. "He knew my voice meant treats, and he put it all together. That's when I knew he still remembered me."

Sam Rubin cannot make the same claim. Soon after John was retired, Rubin visited him, with carrot in hand. He knew when McAnally called "John," the horse came running. "I tried calling 'John,' and nothing," he said. "Finally, he saw the carrot and inched his way over. He ate the carrot, then turned around, took a crap, and walked away. That's my relationship with John Henry."

That same Derby Week of 1990, the announcement was made that John Henry had been elected into racing's Hall of Fame. To make the occasion even more special, McAnally was elected in as well. "I was so choked up on the stand, I couldn't even say the things I wanted to say," McAnally said. "I just thank God that John was around to get me there, because only God knows where horses like that come from."

In December of 1988, Wes Lanter had left the Horse Park to return to working with stallions. He eventually wound up at Three Chimneys Farm, taking care of Seattle Slew and then was hired as stallion manager at Overbrook Farm.

In 1990 John made a new friend, who would become as close to him as anyone in his life. Rosemary Honerkamp was hired as stud groom, beginning a special relationship that would last until her departure in 1997.

"Their relationship was something right out of *Black Beauty*," said Tammy Siters, who takes care of John while sharing duties with ten-year Horse Park veteran Cathy Roby. "John truly loved Rosemary and never once even looked cross-eyed at her."

One day the manager of the Breeds Barn, Peggy

Carroll, came up to help out, and went to John's stall to take him outside. John didn't particularly care for her and wanted nothing to do with her, so he laid down in his stall, with his body right up against the door so that she couldn't get in. When Honerkamp came in the barn to see what was going on, Carroll said to her, "You want that horse, you'll have to get him yourself," with a few expletives thrown in. Honerkamp went up to the stall door and simply said, "John, get up," and he jumped to his feet. She put on the lead shank and he was a perfect gentleman.

Honerkamp had become friends with Phil Marino, who suggested she apply for the job at the Horse Park. She eventually became manager of the stallion barn, while building up a close friendship with John Henry.

"John seemed to like women better than men," she said. "If you walked in his stall and talked nicely to him, he was fine. But you never told John to do anything. You asked him. If it was okay with him, everything was fine, and if it wasn't, you might as well just back up and go on and do something else."

Honerkamp also knew right away when something was wrong with John. "Anytime he was sick, his whole attitude changed," she said. "He'd let you know he was sick. He'd nuzzle up against you and practically put his head in your pocket, as if he were asking you to help him. He was just like a big baby. And he sure loved his treats. I would always go in his stall with a carrot or an apple or a mint. Mr. McAnally would come visit him with his arms loaded down with apples and carrots, and he'd just cry when he saw John. That horse really touched him. It's amazing how many people John has touched, not so much for what he did on the track, but by just being John."

In addition to his usual treats, John has been known to eat pizza and drink coffee on occasion, with cream and sugar, of course. And then there is the Carrot Lady, the title bestowed upon Emma Dailey, a Lexington resident who has visited John on a regular basis since the day he arrived. Whenever Dailey shows up, John knows it's carrot heaven.

"He's the love of my life," said Dailey, who visits John religiously every two or three weeks. "My daughter says I have a shrine to him. I went to the Horse Park on "John Henry Day" back in 1984. I was with Jose when he said goodbye to him and we cried together. I

promised John then that I'd never forget him, and I haven't. I started bringing him carrots and it just ballooned from there. The girls tell me they know I'm coming from the way John is acting. We just have this communication between us."

Despite his age, John can still be plenty ornery. When Siters first started working at the Hall of Champions as a seasonal employee in 1996, she wouldn't work with John. "I'd been around a lot of horses," she said, "but John was the only one who ever scared me. When someone new came, he'd always pick on them and test them. After I came back for good in April of 1998, I said, 'This is ridiculous. I'm not going to let this horse scare me. I have to get over the fear and deal with it.'

"After all, I really did like the horse. I just showed him he can't run me out of his stall. If you hold your ground and don't act afraid, then he doesn't want to play the game any more, especially if he doesn't have the upper hand."

But one day in October 1998, Siters got the scare of her life. Something set John off, and when she went in the stall to get him, he charged her, then reared up and went right for her face. "I saw my life flash before my eyes," she said. "Luckily, I had the lead shank and I smacked him over the shoulder with it. He went to the corner of the stall and just shook all over. You could see the whites of his eyes. He was petrified. He thought it was me who was now trying to kill him. I felt so bad, I had one of the girls bring in some mints for me to give him. And this is a horse who had just tried to kill me.

"It's like he has a split personality. He wants to be good, and there is a real good side to him, but sometimes that evil John just has to come out."

Another incident convinced Siters that John actually understood every word she said. It was during the winter, and she was cleaning John's stall. "He was being a real pain in the butt, chasing me around the stall and biting. Finally, I said, 'John, I've had enough of this. Go outside in your paddock and I'll tell when your stall is done and when you can come back in.' He just walked out the door and watched me. I left the back door open and finished cleaning his stall. Then I went out and brought the tractor in and loaded everything, and went upstairs and threw the hay down. I noticed all the other horses were inside eating except John. I went to his stall, and there's John still standing at the open door looking in. I had forgotten to tell him it was okay to come back in. I said, 'Okay, you can come back in now,' and he just came waltzing right in the door. I've never been around a horse like him."

Siters and Roby have stood up to the battle, despite John breaking Siters' nose with a cow kick and breaking Roby's toe by stepping on it. Once, when a Japanese television crew came to do a feature on John, Roby went to get him, and he bit her thumb. "I brought John out and showed him, and I'm standing there on Japanese TV with blood running down my elbow," she said.

John also hates medicine, and whenever he's given a dewormer, which is a pasty substance, he keeps it in his mouth for hours and refuses to swallow it. One time, Roby took him out to show him several hours after he had been given the medication. "John was standing in the ring," she said, "and all of a sudden, he blows this wormer all over the audience."

John's typical day during the show season, which is March 15 until October 31, consists of coming in at 8 a.m. and having breakfast, then getting bathed and groomed for the 10:15 a.m. showing. After the show, he takes his morning nap and then gets ready for the 1 p.m. show. At 3 o'clock, he gets brushed for the final show at 3:30. Then, it's back out in his paddock until the following morning. During the winter months, John is pretty much on his own and has Mondays and Tuesdays completely to himself.

John is still so sound that when he had precautionary X-rays taken in 2000, the vet was so amazed at how clean they were, he said he could take the X-rays over to Keeneland and pass them off as belonging to one of the yearlings. He told Siters and Roby he had never seen anything like it in such an old horse.

One particular morning in February, 2001, neither Siters nor Roby could get John in. "He was dashing across his paddock and jumping with all four feet off the ground and nickering," Siters said. "He was just feeling so good. We tried for thirty minutes, then gave up."

John's youthful exuberance is something he'll likely take to his grave. Perhaps that was one of the reasons he remained great for so long. Because Balzac was defeated by John on more than one occasion it seems

appropriate to quote the horse's two-legged namesake, who said, "There is no such thing as a great talent without great will-power."

Was John Henry born a great talent? Was he singled out for greatness by higher forces? Did Ron McAnally tap into something he never dreamed possible by mere acts of kindness and training skills? Those are things we'll never know. In all likelihood, Balzac was correct. John Henry possessed great willpower, and it was that unrelenting determination that enabled him to use all the physical qualities the scientists and experts said he possessed. In short, he willed himself to be great.

John Henry's life is woven like some great tapestry, not only of the Turf, but of the stage, where one human drama after another was played out. To those who live in the shadow of John's past, there no longer are feelings of what might have been. They are content with the knowledge that for a brief moment in time true greatness passed their way and that perhaps they helped move it along toward its place in history.

Sam Rubin kept his word. He took his one shot and then basically called it quits. At age eighty-six, he spends a good deal of his time at his country club in Palm Beach, Florida. But recently, he began to dabble again, buying a couple of horses in partnership with several members of his club. And after seventeen years, Rubin showed he hasn't lost that Midas touch. On March 2, 2001, his filly O K to Dance won the listed Gaily Gaily Stakes at Gulfstream for her first career stakes victory.

Ron McAnally continued his Hall of Fame career, saddling Eclipse champions Bayakoa, Paseana, Tight Spot, and Northern Spur. He won the Breeders' Cup Distaff twice with Bayakoa and once with Paseana, and the Breeders' Cup Turf with Northern Spur. He also took home two more Eclipse Awards as leading trainer in 1991 and 1992. Eduardo Inda went out on his own, and in 2000, trained champion older female Riboletta. Lewis Cenicola took out his trainer's license in 1985 and formed a public stable the following year. He has won dozens of minor stakes, but still is looking for that one big horse. Cenicola's top groom is none other than Jose Mercado, and one of his exercise riders is Tony Rubalcada, whom he had replaced as John's rider in the fall of 1980.

And at the Kentucky Horse Park, just miles from where he was born, the radiant spirit that is John Henry still glows after all these years. Now age twenty-six, he remains, in Bob Dylan's words, forever young.

JOHN HENRY's
PEDIGREE

		Princequillo, 1940	Prince Rose / Cosquilla
	Prince Blessed, 1957		
OLE BOB BOWERS, b, 1963		Dog Blessed, 1941	**Bull Dog** / Blessed Again
		Bull Lea, 1935	**Bull Dog** / Rose Leaves
	Blue Jeans, 1950		
JOHN HENRY, bay gelding, 1975		Blue Grass, 1944	Blue Larkspur / Camelot
		Balladier, 1932	Black Toney / Blue Warbler
	Double Jay, 1944		
ONCE DOUBLE, dkb/br, 1967		Broomshot, 1926	Whisk Broom II / Centre Shot
		Intent, 1948	War Relic / Liz F.
	Intent One, 1955		
		Dusty Legs, 1945	Mahmoud / Dustemall

194

JOHN HENRY's RACE RECORD

John Henry — **b. g. 1975, by Ole Bob Bowers (Prince Blessed)–Once Double, by Double Jay** — **Lifetime record: 83 39 15 9 $6,597,947**

Own.– Dotsam Stable
Br.– Golden Chance Farm Inc (Ky)
Tr.– Ronald McAnally

13Oct84- 8Med	fm 1⅜Ⓣ	:46^4 1:11 1:35^1 2:13	3↑ Ballantine H 900k	4	8	8^9	5^{3½}	3^{1½}	1^{2¾}	McCarron CJ	126	*.60	100-06	JohnHnry126^{2¾}Who'sforDinner115^{hd}Win120^1	Came out,clear	12
22Sep84- 8Bel	fm 1½Ⓣ	:48^4 1:13 2:01^3 2:25^1	3↑ Turf Classic-G1	4	1	1^{1½}	1^{½}	1^{½}	1^{nk}	McCarron CJ	126	*1.00	98-10	JohnHnry126^{nk}Win126^{4}Majesty'sPrnc126^{hd}	Strong handling	6
26Aug84- 9AP	fm 1¼Ⓣ	:48^2 1:12^2 1:37^2 2:01^2	3↑ Bud Arl Million-G1	6	4	3^{1½}	3^2	1^{hd}	1^{1¾}	McCarron CJ	126	*1.10	87-15	JohnHenry126^{1¾}RoyalHeroine122^{3}GatodelSol126^{no}	Drew out	12
23Jly84- 8Hol	fm 1½Ⓣ	:47^1 1:10^3 1:59^4 2:24^4	3↑ Sunset H-G1	7	5	4^7	3^2	2^1	1^1	McCarron CJ	126	*1.20	96-08	JhnHnry126^{1}LoadtheCannons118^{1½}PairofDeuces113^{nk}	Driving	9
24Jun84- 8Hol	fst 1¼	:47 1:10 1:35 2:00^2	3↑ Hol Gold Cup H-G1	4	4	4^{3½}	3^2	3^2	2^2	McCarron CJ	125	2.60	87-20	DesertWine122^{2}JohnHnry125^{1½}Sari'sDreamer114^{nk}	Game try	8
28May84- 8Hol	fm 1½Ⓣ	:49 1:12^3 2:01^1 2:25	3↑ Hol Inv'l H-G1	1	2	3^{1½}	3^{1½}	3^{nk}	1^{½}	McCarron CJ	126	*.80	95-08	JohnHnry126^{½}GalantVert116^{2¾}LoadtheCannons120^{1¼}	Driving	9
6May84- 8GG	fm 1⅜Ⓣ	:47^2 1:12 1:35^4 2:13	3↑ Golden Gate H-G3	6	3	3^{4½}	2^2	1^{½}	1^2	McCarron CJ	125	*.50	103-09	John Henry125^{2}Silveyville117^{6}Lucence116^6	Slow st.,clear	6
1Apr84- 8SA	fm 1½Ⓣ	:48^2 1:13^2 2:02^2 2:26^4	3↑ San Luis Rey-G1	4	2	2^1	1^{½}	2^{½}	3^{¾}	McCarron CJ	126	1.60	80-17	Interco126^{nk}Gato del Sol126^{½}John Henry126^{3½}	Weakened	10
4Mar84- 8SA	fst 1¼	:45^3 1:10 1:35 2:00^3	4↑ S Anita H-G1	10	7	7^{6¼}	4^5	5^6	5^8	McCarron CJ	127	*2.40	78-17	Interco121^{2¾}Journey at Sea117^{1½}Gato del Sol117^{1¾}		12
	Stumble after start															
11Dec83- 8Hol	gd 1⅜Ⓣ	:49^4 1:15^3 1:40 2:16^3	3↑ Hol Turf Cup-G1	4	2	2^{2½}	1^{½}	2^{hd}	1^{½}	McCarron CJ	126	*1.50	72-27	John Henry126^{½}Zalataia123^{1½}Palikaraki126^{1¼}	Came again	12
13Nov83- 8SA	gd 1½Ⓣ	:47^2 1:13^1 2:03^4 2:29^1	3↑ Oak Tree Inv'l-G1	2	5	3^1	4^{3½}	3^1	2^{½}	McCarron CJ	126	*.80	68-31	Zalataia123^{½}JohnHnry126^{1½}LoadthCnnons122^{3½}	Held gamely	9
15Oct83- 8Bel	fst 1½	:48 1:12^3 2:01 2:26^1	3↑ J C Gold Cup-G1	7	6	5^3	4^5	5^5	5^{6¾}	McCarron CJ	126	2.90	82-14	Slew o'Gold121^{3}Highland Blade126^{nk}Bounding Basque121^{1½}		11
	Weakened															
28Aug83- 9AP	gd 1¼Ⓣ	:50^3 1:15^4 1:41^3 2:04^2	3↑ Arl Million-G1	13	3	2^1	2^{½}	2^{½}	2^{nk}	McCarron CJ	126	*1.40	72-28	Tolomeo118^{nk}JohnHenry126^{½}Nijinsky'sSecret126^2	Sharp try	14
4Jly83- 8Hol	fm 1⅛Ⓣ	:49 1:13 1:36^3 1:48^2	3↑ American H-G2	1	3	3^3	2^{1½}	2^{½}	1^{1¼}	McCarron CJ	127	2.10	88-12	JohnHenry127^{1¼}PrinceFlorimund120^{½}Tonzarun114^{no}	Driving	8
28Nov82♦ Tokyo(Jpn)	fm*1½ⓉLH	2:27	3↑ Japan Cup-G1 Stk801000						13^8	Shoemaker W	126	*.90		Half Iced121^{nk}All Along117^{nk}April Run121^1	Prominent to stretch	15
13Nov82- 6Med	gd 1¼	:47^3 1:12^1 1:37 2:01^2	3↑ Med Cup H-G2	2	5	3^{7½}	4^{4¼}	3^{5½}	3^{5¾}	Shoemaker W	129	*1.10	89-15	Mehmet118^{1¼}ThirtyEghtPcs113^{4½}JhnHnry129^{4½}	Lacked a bid	9
31Oct82- 8SA	fm 1½Ⓣ	:47^2 1:10^3 1:59^3 2:24	3↑ Oak Tree Inv'l-G1	6	4	4^4	2^{1½}	2^{½}	1^{2½}	Shoemaker W	126	1.40	95-05	John Henry126^{2½}Craelius122^{1½}Regalberto126^2	Drew clear	7
17Oct82- 8SA	fm 1¼Ⓣ	:47^1 1:11 1:34^3 1:58^3	3↑ C F Burke H-G2	6	3	3^{1½}	4^2	4^{2¾}	4^{1½}	Shoemaker W	129	*.80	92-06	Mehmet117^{hd}Craelius114^{1½}It's the One124^{no}	Evenly	7
28Mar82- 8SA	fm 1½Ⓣ	:46^2 1:10^2 2:00 2:24	4↑ San Luis Rey-G1	3	3	3^3	3^3	4^{3½}	3^{4¾}	Shoemaker W	126	*.50	90-05	Perrault126^{3¼}Exploded126^{1½}John Henry126^{no}	Evenly	5
7Mar82- 8SA	fst 1¼	:45 1:09 1:34^2 1:59	4↑ S Anita H-G1	9	8	9^{13}	5^{1¼}	2^{½}	2no	Shoemaker W	130	*1.30	94-07	[D]Perrault126^{no}JhnHenry130^{3¼}It'stheOne123^{nk}	Impeded end	11
	Placed first by disqualification															
6Dec81- 8Hol	fm 1½Ⓣ	:49 1:13 2:03 2:26^4	3↑ Hol Turf Cup 550k	5	1	1^2	1^1	3^{½}	4^2	Shoemaker W	126	*.40	84-11	Providential II126^{nk}Queen to Conquer123^{1½}Goldiko126^{nk}		10
	Weakened;Previously trained by Victor J. Nickerson															
8Nov81- 8SA	fm 1½Ⓣ	:47^2 1:10^2 1:59^3 2:23^2	3↑ Oak Tree Inv'l-G1	4	3	1^{½}	1^{½}	2^{hd}	1^{nk}	Shoemaker W	126	*.40	98-02	John Henry126^{nk}Spence Bay126^{4½}The Bart126^{no}	Driving	7
10Oct81- 8Bel	fst 1½	:48 1:12^3 2:02^1 2:28^2	3↑ J C Gold Cup-G1	8	5	4^{2½}	2^1	1^{1½}	1^{hd}	Shoemaker W	126	*3.10	78-14	JohnHenry126^{hd}PeatMoss126^{¾}Relaxing123^{hd}	Bore in,driving	11
	Previously trained by Ronald McAnally															
30Aug81- 6AP	sf 1¼Ⓣ	:50^1 1:15^3 1:42^2 2:07^3	3↑ Arl Million 1000k	12	8	8^{6½}	5^6	3^1	1no	Shoemaker W	126	*1.10e	- -	John Henry126^{no}The Bart126^{2¼}Madam Gay117^{½}	Just up	12
	Previously trained by Victor J. Nickerson															
11Jly81- 8Bel	fm 1½Ⓣ	:49^4 1:14^2 2:03 2:26^4	3↑ Sword Dancer-G3	3	3	3^{1½}	1^1	1^{1½}	1^{3½}	Shoemaker W	126	*.30	90-13	JohnHnry126^{3½}PassingZone126^{1¾}PeatMoss126^{1¾}	Ridden out	5
	Previously trained by Ronald McAnally															
14Jun81- 8Hol	fst 1¼	:45^3 1:09^3 1:34^4 2:00^2	3↑ Hol Gold Cup H-G1	7	7	6^{6¼}	6^{5¾}	4^{6½}	4^{2¾}	Pincay L Jr	130	*1.20	86-16	[D]Caterman120^{hd}Eleven Stitches122^{2½}Super Moment117^{nk}		10
	Wide late															

Copyrighted © 2000 by Daily Racing Form, Inc. Reprinted from the book "Champions" (DRF Press)

17May81- 8Hol	fm	1½Ⓣ	:51^1 1:15^1 2:04 2:27^4	3↑ Hol Inv'l H-G1	5	2	2½	2½	1½	1¾	Pincay L Jr	130	*.40	81-12	John Henry130¾Caterman122hdGalaxy Libra118nk	Driving	7
29Mar81- 8SA	fm	1½Ⓣ	:46 1:10^4 2:00 2:25^1	4↑ San Luis Rey-G1	1	2	2^{1½}	2^2	1hd	1^{2¼}	Pincay L Jr	126	*.20	89-11	John Henry126^{2¼}Obraztsovy126^{1½}Fiestero126hd	Easily	6
8Mar81- 8SA	fst	1¼	:45^2 1:09^2 1:34^1 1:59^2	4↑ S Anita H-G1	3	7	6^{5¼}	2^2	1hd	1^1	Pincay L Jr	128	1.90	92-11	John Henry128^{1}King Go Go117^{1¼}Exploded115no	Driving	11
16Feb81- 8SA	fm	1½Ⓣ	:47^4 1:11^3 1:59 2:24	4↑ San Luis Obispo H-G2	4	1	1^1	1^1	1^{2½}	1^{1½}	Pincay L Jr	127	*.50	95-05	John Henry127^{1½}Galaxy Libra119^{5½}Zor115^{1½}	Ridden out	6
16Nov80- 8SA	fm	1½Ⓣ	:45^4 1:10^1 1:58^2 2:23^2	3↑ Oak Tree Inv-G1	6	5	5^{6½}	6^{6¾}	3^{7½}	1^{1½}	Pincay L Jr	126	*1.50	98-02	John Henry126^{1½}Balzac126½Bold Tropic126nk	Drew clear	10
	Previously trained by Victor J. Nickerson																
25Oct80- 8Aqu	sf	1½Ⓣ	:51^4 1:19^2 2:13 2:39^3	3↑ Turf Classic-G1	4	1	1^2	2^3	2^5	3^8	Pincay L Jr	126	*2.00	35-57	Anifa123^{3}Golden Act126^{5}John Henry126nk	Weakened	8
4Oct80- 8Bel	fst	1½	:49^4 1:15 2:05^1 2:30^1	3↑ J C Gold Cup-G1	3	2	2^1	2½	2^3	2^{5½}	Cordero A Jr	126	*.70	63-19	Temperence Hill121^{5½}John Henry126^{2}Ivory Hunter126^{3¼}		7
	Best of others																
7Sep80- 8Bel	fm	1¼[T]	:48^3 1:12^2 1:36^2 1:59^2	3↑ Brighton Beach H-G3	5	1	1hd	1^{1½}	1^{1½}	1nk	Cordero A Jr	125	*.40	97-15	John Henry125nkPremier Ministre117^{4}Match the Hatch113^3		5
	Driving																
12Jly80- 8Bel	fm	1½Ⓣ	:47 1:11^1 2:01 2:25^1	3↑ Sword Dancer 161k	2	2	2^1	1½	2hd	2^{1¼}	McHargue DG	126	*.80	97-15	Tiller126^{1¼}John Henry126^{5}Sten126^{12}	Gamely	4
14Jun80- 8Bel	fm	1⅜Ⓣ	:47^3 1:11^3 1:35^2 2:13^1	3↑ Bowling Green H-G2	3	1	1½	1hd	1½	2nk	McHargue DG	128	*1.80	96-15	Sten117nkJohn Henry128^{1}Lyphard's Wish120nk	Brushed	9
	Previously trained by Ronald McAnally																
26May80- 8Hol	fm	1½Ⓣ	:48^3 1:12^3 2:01^2 2:25^2	3↑ Hol Inv'l H-G1	4	1	1^4	1^{2½}	1½	1nk	McHargue DG	128	*.90	93-09	John Henry128nkBalzac120^{1½}Go West Young Man117^{2½}		10
	Fully extended																
6Apr80- 8SA	fm	*1¾Ⓣ	:46 1:59^4 2:46^4	4↑ S Juan Capistrano H-G1	3	1	1^2	1^{1½}	1^2	1^{1¼}	McHargue DG	126	*2.20	93-08	John Henry126^{1¼}Fiestero114nkThe Very One113hd	Driving	11
16Mar80- 8SA	fm	1½Ⓣ	:46^4 1:10^4 1:59^2 2:23	4↑ San Luis Rey-G1	3	2	2^1	2½	2½	1^{1½}	McHargue DG	126	6.90	100-00	John Henry126^{1½}Relaunch126noSilver Eagle126no	Drew out	7
23Feb80-10Hia	fm	1½Ⓣ	2:29^2	3↑ Hia Turf Cup H-G2	10	2	3^{1½}	1^1	1^{1½}	1½	McHargue DG	122	2.30	84-22	JohnHenry122½DancingMaster113^{5}IvoryHunter111hd	Driving	10
20Jan80- 8SA	fst	1¼	:47 1:11^3 1:36^4 2:01^3	4↑ San Marcos H-G3	2	1	1^{1½}	1^1	1^1	1^{2½}	McHargue DG	124	*.80	85-17	John Henry124^{2½}El Fantastico113^{2¼}Commemorativo110nk		5
	Handily																
1Jan80- 8SA	gd	1⅛Ⓣ	:48 1:12^1 1:37^1 1:49^4	4↑ San Gabriel H-G3	4	2	2^2	2^{1½}	2½	1hd	McHargue DG	123	*1.70	78-22	John Henry123hdSmasher111^{5}As de Copas117^3	Driving	9
8Dec79- 8BM	fm	1⅛Ⓣ	:47^1 1:11^1 1:36^3 1:49^3	3↑ Bay Meadows H 114k	7	5	4^{4½}	8^{3¾}	1hd	2^{1¼}	McHargue DG	123	2.70	103-00	Leonotis118^{1¼}John Henry123^{4}Capt. Don117½	Held on	14
5Nov79- 8SA	fm	1⅛Ⓣ	:46^1 1:10^2 1:35^2 1:48	3↑ HP Russell H (Div 2) 45k	5	2	1^1	1^1	1^2	1^{3¼}	McHargue DG	122	*.70	87-15	JohnHenry122^{3¼}Rusty Canyon114hdLeonotis117^2	Ridden out	8
14Oct79- 8SA	fm	1¼Ⓣ	:45^4 1:10 1:34^3 1:59^1	3↑ C F Burke H-G2	5	3	2^{1½}	1hd	1hd	2^{1¼}	McHargue DG	118	3.40	90-09	Silver Eagle115^{1¼}John Henry118½Shagbark118^{1¼}	Gamely	9
	Previously trained by Victor J. Nickerson																
10Sep79- 7Bel	fm	1 1/16Ⓣ	:24 :47 1:11 1:41^4	3↑ Alw 30000	2	1	1^3	1^{1½}	1^2	1^2	Santiago A	117	1.90	87-17	John Henry117^{2}Silent Cal117½Waya119no	Ridden out	4
22Aug79- 7Sar	fm	1⅛Ⓣ	:46^2 1:11^1 1:34^3 1:46^2	3↑ Alw 27000	3	1	1^{1½}	1^{1½}	1^{1½}	1^{2½}	Santiago A	115	*1.40	95-13	John Henry115^{2½}Told114¾Poison Ivory122^4	Driving	7
29Jly79- 7Pen	sly	1 1/16	:23^2 :47^1 1:11^4 1:44^3	3↑ Capital City H 33k	7	5	4^{1½}	3^1	4^{1¼}	4^2	Santiago A	113	2.30	81-23	Horatius118nkTanthem112^{1½}Shy Jester115nk	Hung	7
14Jly79- 8Bel	fm	1 1/16Ⓣ	:23^3 :47 1:10^4 1:41^3	3↑ Sword Dancer 57k	2	1	2hd	2^1	2^2	2^{2½}	Santiago A	119	5.70	85-11	Darby Creek Road119^{2½}John Henry119^{4}Poison Ivory119^{1¾}		8
	Best of others																
6Jly79- 6Atl	fm	1 1/16Ⓣ	:23 :46^2 1:10^2 1:41^1	3↑ Sunrise H 35k	2	2	2^{1½}	1½	1hd	2^{2¼}	McCauley WH	111	*1.50	98-09	Chati118^{2¼}John Henry111½Fed Funds115^4	Tired	11
24Jun79-10Suf	fst	1⅛	:45^3 1:10 1:36 1:48^3	3↑ Mass H-G3	9	4	6^{8¾}	8^{4¼}	9^6	10^{8½}	Borden DA	108	6.90	89-21	Island Sultan110¾Western Front113½Quiet Jay116^{1½}	Tired	13
5Jun79- 8Mth	fst	1	:23^2 :47 1:11^4 1:37^3	4↑ Alw 18000	1	3	2hd	1^3	1^8	1^{14}	McCauley WH	119	*.90	85-23	John Henry119^{14}Thou Fool119noM.A.'s Date113^{1¾}	Driving	7
26May79- 6Mth	fst	6f	:22 :44^3 1:10^4	4↑ Alw 16000	4	4	5^{3½}	4^{1¾}	2^{1½}	2½	McCauley WH	117	6.90	85-19	ReallyandTruly117½JohnHnry117^{1¼}Kintla'sFolly115^3	Gamely	7
	Previously trained by Robert A. Donato																

JOHN HENRY's RACE RECORD CONTINUED

29Oct78-6Pen	fm 1 1/16Ⓣ				1:412		Chcltetwn H (Div 2) 22k	5	2	21	1½	12	11	Broussard R	124		*.70	--	John Henry1241Scythian Gold1166½Berlin's Burning1122	Ridden out	7
15Oct78-5SA	fm 1¼Ⓣ	:453	1:094	1:342	1:59	3↑	C F Burke H (Div 1)-G2	2	1	1hd	1hd	44	65	Baltazar C	117		2.80	87-08	Star of Erin II113noImproviser1152¾Mr. Redoy1181¼	Tired	9
8Oct78-8SA	fm 1⅛Ⓣ	:46	1:102	1:351	1:474		Volante H-G3	6	4	42	41	31½	3½	Baltazar C	122		*2.30	87-12	WaysideStation117noAprilAxe120½JohnHenry1222	In close	11
16Sep78-8AP	gd 1 1/16Ⓣ	:241	:484	1:131	1:454		Round Table H-G3	6	1	11	13	18	112	Amy J	121		*.50	80-30	JhnHnry12112GordieH.109noBringtheMoney111no	Ridden out	9
9Sep78-5Bel	fm 7fⓉ	:232	:46	1:093	1:22	3↑	Alw 21000	1	1	11½	11½	11	11½	Amy J	113		3.60	94-09	John Henry1131½Gab Bag1174Proud Arion1171¼	Hard ridden	8
18Aug78-7Sar	fm 1 1/16Ⓣ	:251	:49	1:12	1:41	3↑	Alw 23000	7	2	2½	2hd	44	47¼	Amy J	112		5.10	85-08	Blue Baron1172¼Quip1141Stir the Embers1194	Weakened	8
8Aug78-7Sar	gd 7f	:223	:444	1:081	1:202	3↑	Alw 23000	2	2	31½	24	38	514	Santiago A	113		2.90	89-04	DarbyCreekRoad11311Liberal117¾GoldenReserve117¾	Tired	6
29Jly78-8Bel	fm 1 1/16Ⓣ	:233	:46	1:103	1:41		Lexington H-G2	5	1	12½	12	11	2hd	Santiago A	112		5.90	91-11	Mac Diarmida126hdJohn Henry1124¼Ashikaga110hd	Gamely	9
19Jly78-8Bel	fm 1Ⓣ	:24	:473	1:104	1:351		Hill Prince H 37k	5	1	2hd	2hd	2½	21½	Santiago A	111		3.60	92-12	DarbyCreekRd1211½JhnHnry1112ScythianGold1116	Gamely	9
1Jly78-8Mth	fm 1 1/16Ⓣ	:232	:47	1:11	1:432		Lamplighter H-G3	4	2	2hd	1hd	1½	3½	Santiago A	112		*1.50	83-16	North Course112nkHoratius114nkJohnHenry112no	Weakened	9
25Jun78-6Bel	hd 1 1/16Ⓣ	:232	:47	1:102	1:411	3↑	Alw 18000	2	5	62½	52	42	1nk	Santiago A	112		3.40	90-07	John Henry112nkTurn of Coin1171¾Valinsky1171¾	Driving	9
1Jun78-7Bel	fm 1 1/16Ⓣ	:231	:47	1:11	1:413		Clm 35000	1	2	21	1½	17	114	Santiago A	117		3.30	88-12	JhnHnry11714ContinentalCousin117¾CptnPeter1132¼	Driving	10
21May78-2Aqu	fst 6f	:224	:471		1:123		Clm 25000	4	4	32½	1½	11	12½	Santiago A	117		12.30	80-27	John Henry1172½Please See Me1171½Orfanik115nk	Driving	9
	Previously owned and trained by H. Snowden Jr																				
11Apr78-7Kee	fst 6f	:22	:45	:59	1:093		Alw 8500	4	4	47½	46	48½	49½	McKnight J	113		6.40	84-15	Johnny Blade1074½Schottis112½Jester Beau1154½	No mishap	6
	Previously owned by D. Lingo & C. Madere; previously trained by Phil Marino																				
22Mar78-9FG	fst 6f	:23	:47		1:12		Clm 25000	7	6	78	89	64¾	34	Copling D	114		25.10	81-16	Kim's Red1142Bunny Wag1122John Henry1141	Rallied	9
22Feb78-9FG	fst 6f	:223	:463		1:113		Clm 20000	11	2	98¾	98¾	1015	1020	Elmer D	112	b	19.10	67-19	AdriaticEditions1144Bladesville113½Kim'sRed1141	Outrun	11
15Feb78-6FG	fst 6f	:22	:462		1:113		Clm 25000	5	5	85¼	61¼	63¾	66¼	Guajardo A	112	b	4.90	81-19	MercrCounty1121½Gen'sLTroy1121AdrtcEdtons1141	No mishap	8
4Feb78-6FG	fst 1 40	:252	:493	1:151	1:43		Alw 7500	2	9	84¾	83½	53¼	55¾	Guajardo A	112		17.10	72-23	HogTown114¾TrafficWarning114hdSmokePole1092½	No mishap	10
23Jan78-8FG	gd 1 40	:241	:473	1:131	1:424		Alw 7500	7	4	42¾	52¾	86¾	86½	Guajardo A	112		22.20	72-24	CabriniGreen117½DayTimeTudor1121As in Elbow112no	Tired	9
31Dec77-9FG	fst 6f	:22	:46		1:121		Sugar Bowl H 50k	4	12	127¾	127½	1210	1114	McKnight J	113		16.80	70-21	CabriniGreen122½CouponRate113¾SpecialHonr1101¼	Outrun	12
17Dec77-6FG	gd 6f	:223	:472		1:122		©Alw 7000	1	6	64¼	62¾	53¾	31¼	McKnight J	113		7.90	82-18	CabriniGreen1201¼CouponRate113hdJohnHenry113hd	Rallied	12
3Dec77-8FG	fst 6f	:222	:462		1:114		Alw 7000	1	7	75¾	54	51¾	43½	McKnight J	120		8.70	82-19	DragonTamer1171½TrafficWarnng1171¼HogTwn117¾	Rallied	11
19Nov77-9FG	fst 6f	:221	:464		1:124		©Sthern Hospitality 19k	8	12	105	63¼	64¼	59	Guajardo A	122		9.60	72-22	CbrniGreen1144MajesticSpiral1122½HogTown112hd	Late bid	12
5Sep77-11EvD	sly 6f	:232	:47	1:01	1:142		Lafayette Futurity 86k	1	6		45	32½	1hd	Guajardo A	120		5.10	79-26	JohnHenry120hdLilLizaJayne1171SoundNote1203½	Driving	12
25Aug77-7EvD	gd 6f	:223	:462	1:002	1:13		Sp Wt 2700	8	5		33	32	2½	Guajardo A	120		4.10	85-21	Note to Mame117½John Henry1203Tudor Luck117hd		9
6Aug77-7EvD	sly 5f	:224	:483		1:001		Alw 2400	4	9		54½	1hd	13	Guajardo A	120		3.00	82-19	John Henry1203Motor Dude1201½Bell's Chief1174	Driving	12
29Jly77-8JnD	fst *6f	:233	:473	1:02	1:152		Handicap 7500	9	9	-	-	-	-	Munster L	102		3.90	--	RunLikeHeck1191CapGardnr1072HarktheLedr1102	Lost rider	9
2Jly77-6JnD	sly 5f	:23	:481		1:011		Alw 4500	2	5		42	33	23	Spiehler G	116		*2.60	81-19	KindaNughty1133JhnHnry1161MossBluffKd1152	Bid,weakened	7
7Jun77-8JnD	fst 4f	:22			:471		Alw 3500	4	6		59	55½	31	Spiehler G	120		14.60	89-11	DancngMeadw109¾DancingJudge120nkJhnHnry1201	Rallied	8
20May77-1JnD	fst 4f	:23			:481		Md Sp Wt	1	7		54½	34	1no	Spiehler G	120		1.70	85-15	JhnHnry120noYouSexyThing1172Ricky'sChoice112¾	Driving	8

Index

Photo Credits

Cover photo: (The Blood-Horse)

Page 1: John Henry winning 1982 Oak Tree Invitational (Four Footed Fotos); John Henry head shot (Patricia McQueen)

Page 2: Ole Bob Bowers (courtesy California Thoroughbred); Prince Blessed (The Blood-Horse); Double Jay (The Blood-Horse); John Henry as weanling (Golden Chance Farm photo)

Page 3: Verna and Robert Lehmann (Winants Bros.); Fred Lehmann (Milt Toby); Golden Chance Farm (Milt Toby); Golden Chance residence and bell tower (The Blood-Horse)

Page 4: John Henry's first win (Jefferson Downs); John Callaway with John Henry (courtesy Jean Callaway); Bubba Snowden Jr. (Anne M. Eberhardt)

Page 5: Bill Shoemaker on John Henry (Milt Toby); Darrel McHargue on John (Lydia A. Williams); Laffit Pincay Jr. on John (Santa Anita); Chris McCarron (The Blood-Horse)

Page 6: Bobby Donato (Tom Hall); Lefty Nickerson (Adam Coglianese); Ron McAnally and John Henry (Katey Barrett)

Page 7: Sam and Dorothy Rubin at Eclipse Awards (Jim Raftery); Rubin leading in John Henry (Bob Coglianese)

Page 8: Eduardo Inda (Del Mar); Lewis Cenicola on John Henry (Lydia A. Williams); Jose Mercado with John Henry (Janice Wilkman)

Page 9: John Henry after winning the H. P. Russell (Vic Stein); Winning the Round Table (Arlington Park); Winning the Chocolatetown (Penn National)

Page 10-11: Winning the San Marcos (Santa Anita); Winning the Hialeah Turf Cup (Jim Raftery); Winning the San Juan Capistrano (Santa Anita); Winning the 1980 Oak Tree Invitational (Santa Anita)

Page 12: Winning the Hollywood Invitational (Hollywood Park); Winning the Santa Anita Handicap (Santa Anita); Winning the San Luis Obispo (Santa Anita)

Page 13: Winning the Sword Dancer (Bob Coglianese); Winning the 1981 Arlington Million (Arlington Park); Post-Arlington Million (Manny Grossman)

Page 14: John Henry and his fans (Rayetta Burr); Winning the Jockey Club Gold Cup (Bob Coglianese); Winning the 1982 Santa Anita Handicap (Four Footed Fotos); Winning the American Handicap (Hollywood Park)

Page 15: Winning the 1984 Arlington Million (Dan Johnson); Winning the Turf Classic (Dan Johnson); Winning the Scotch Classic (Jim Raftery)

Page 16: John Henry with Gov. Collins; With Wes Lanter ; With Ron McAnally (all by Anne M. Eberhardt); Arlington Park statue (Judy Marchman)

ABOUT THE
AUTHOR

Steve Haskin is an award-winning Turf writer and national correspondent for *The Blood-Horse*, the leading Thoroughbred industry weekly. Haskin spent twenty-nine years with *Daily Racing Form* and became known for his insightful coverage of the Triple Crown races. In 1997 Haskin won the Red Smith Award for best Kentucky Derby advance story and the David Woods Award for best Preakness story.

He has written two other books: *Dr. Fager*, the second volume in the Thoroughbred Legends series, and *Baffert: Dirt Road to the Derby*, which he co-authored with trainer Bob Baffert. Haskin has written for many publications, including *The Thoroughbred Record*, *The Backstretch*, *Pacemaker International*, *The British Racehorse*, *Louisiana Horse*, *Stud & Stable*, and *The Sporting Chronicle*. He has also provided research for many book projects as well as to ABC-TV. He lives in Hamilton Square, New Jersey, with his wife and daughter.

Forthcoming titles
in the

THOROUGHBRED Legends®

series:

Personal Ensign

Sunday Silence

Ruffian

Swaps

Affirmed/Alydar

Available titles

Man o' War

Dr. Fager

Citation

Go for Wand

Seattle Slew

Forego

Native Dancer

Nashua

Spectacular Bid

www.thoroughbredlegends.com